Bethlehem 2000

A Guide to Bethlehem and its Surroundings

D1396241

Sawsan & Qustandi Shomali

FLAMM DRUCK
WAGENER GMBH

Acknowledgment

Special thanks go to many friends who have contributed their valuable time, expertise and advice. Our gratitude goes to: O. Massalha, Director of the Coordination Unit for Assistance to the Palestinian People (UNESCO).

H. J. Wischnewski, President of Städte-Partnerschaft Bethlehem-Cologne.

Latin Seminary (Beit Jala), Christian Information Center (Jerusalem), Bethlehem University, Ministry of Tourism, Tantour Ecumenical Institute, Bethlehem Municipality, The Old Bethlehem Home, Unesco office in Bethlehem, Maha Saca (Center for Palestinian Costumes), Rev. Dr. Betty Jane Bailly, Br. Robert Daszkiewicz, FSC. Professor Bret Wallach, Dr. Basil Rishmawi, Professor Marsha Mihok, Jay Stafford, George Samour and Dr. Khalil Rishmawi.

Much gratitude goes to photographers: Jerome de Baeque, Nabil Da'iq, Ra'id Shomali & Imad Attrash.

HELP US UPDATE

Any suggestions, comments or corrections toward the next edition would be much appreciated.

Send them along to:

Sawsan Shomali, P.O.Box. 100, Doha Street, Beit Sahour, West Bank. Telfax: 972-2- 6473957.
E-Mail: sshomali @bethlehem.edu. or
Dr. Qustandi Shomali, Bethlehem University, P.O.Box 9, Bethlehem, West Bank.Fax: 9722744440, Tel: 97226473957, E-Mail: qshomali@bethlehem.edu. or
Flamm Druck Wagener GmbH, Käthe-Kollwitz-Straße 9, 51545 Waldbröl, P.O. Box 3271, 51532 Waldbröl, Tel: 02291 4005, Fax 02291 4500, Germany.

Front Cover: Panoramic view of the Old Center in Bethlehem.

Back Cover: Traditional Bethlehem wedding dress. Photo by Jerome de Baecque for Bethlehem 2000 Photographic Exhibition.

© 1. Auflage 1997 · ISBN-Nr. 3-9802690-8-6
VERLAGSGESELLSCHAFT FLAMM DRUCK WAGENER GMBH
Satz - Litho - Druck: Flamm Druck Wagener GmbH, 51545 Waldbröl
Buchbinderei: Schiffmann, 51405 Bergisch Gladbach

Foreword

This is the first tourist guide about Bethlehem and its surroundings published in a separate volume. I am happy for the unexpected circumstances that led to its publication. In fact, I had the chance to meet the authors who were working on the book, through Dr. Basil Rischmaui, born in Bethlehem, but is practicing medicine in Morsbach, Germany. He is also a member of the administrative committee of Städte Partnerschaft Bethlehem-Cologne.

Hence, the idea of printing and publishing the book in different languages in Flamm Druck Wagener GmbH in Waldbröl, Germany, was born. I was pleased with the idea, although printing the book in German, English, French, Italien and Arabic is quite a challenge.

The author, Qustandi Shomali, is a professor of Comparative Literature at Bethlehem University. He obtained his university degrees from Algeria, Canada and France. He published many articles and books about various aspects of life in his native country (Palestine). Sawsan Shomali is also a lecturer at Bethlehem University, she worked jointly with her husband on preparing this guide. She was the reader, critic, and writer of many sections of the book such as the chapter on Palestinian food.

The Town of Bethlehem, known all over the world as the place were Jesus was born, is regarded as one of the most important pilgrimage sites in the world. Every year, millions of pilgrims and tourists visit the Church of Nativity, the Grottoes and the Shepherds' Fields. The year 2000, a holy year, will mark the bimillenary of the Nativity. In order to commemorate an event of such importance to all mankind, a great number of tourists and pilgrims will visit the town. I hope that the pictures and texts in this Guide will be an incentive for many people to visit Bethlehem. It will be a good companion as it includes complete and accurate information.

I should be most thankful and grateful to the authors whose deep research and efforts resulted in producing this fulfilling book.

Waldbröl　　　　　　　　　　*Werner Wagener*
August 1997　　　　　　　　*Flamm Druck Wagener GmbH*

Introduction

No town in the world has such a joyous history or exalted status as Bethlehem. The Magi brought gold, frankincense and myrrh from the East to the humble manger in a stable and knelt down and worshipped the child who was born there.

Bethlehem, the birthplace of Jesus Christ, is three times holy, being revered by the followers of the three revealed religions. It contains the shrine of Rachel, the mother of the patriarch Joseph, who was buried on the way to Bethlehem, and it is here that the Prophet Muhammed prayed on his way to Jerusalem. He is reported as having said, "When I was taken on the Midnight Journey to Jerusalem, Gabriel took me to Bethlehem, saying, 'Alight and pray two *raq'as,* for here is the birthplace of your brother Jesus, *peace be upon him,*' and then I was taken to the Rock".

Surely a place so holy is a treasure which all humanity should be proud of and seek to protect. Therefore, a handy book that relates the history of Bethlehem, pointing out a wealth of memorable details and conveying the spell that Bethlehem has cast on the human mind for centuries, is necessary.

Compared to other cities and towns in Palestine, Bethlehem is a relatively quiet place. Despite all the crises and sufferings it went through at various times in history, it was able to survive and attract a huge number of pilgrims and tourists of different nationalities and beliefs.

Moreover, Bethlehem has developed to meet the needs of its local people and visitors. Modern developments safeguard the town original features. It is still a unique holy city, cherished and treasured by thousands of people not only at Christmas but all year round.

This book is a humble attempt to bring Bethlehem and its surrounding region to each visitor in pictures and text. It covers the holy sites and archeological remains along with a full historical, religious, and cultural context.

We did our best to provide the visitor with accurate information, brief and interesting explanation, important facts and practical advice on how to walk through Bethlehem, where to sleep, where and what to eat and all the facts too often discovered too late.

Bethlehem　　　　　　　　　　*Sawsan & Qustandi*
August 1997　　　　　　　　　　　　*Shomali*

Table of Contents

The Nativity Compound

History of Bethlehem

Three thousand years before the birth of Christ, Bethlehem was already known as a settlement. **Canaanite** tribes (including Jebusites, Hittites, Amarites and others) who settled in Palestine, built small cities surrounded by walls for protection against the attacks of raiders. One of these cities was *Beit Lahama* known today as Bethlehem. So, the word Bethlehem derives from *Lahmo* the *Chaldean* god of fertility, which was adopted by the Canaanites as *Lahama.* In accordance with the Canaanite practice of building temples to their gods, they built a temple for *Lahama* on the present mount of the Nativity which overlooked the fertile valleys of the region (*The Shepherds' Fields*). Canaanite wells, ramparts and other structures on the Nativity mount and other sites in Bethlehem clearly establish its Canaanite origin 1000 years before the Hebrew period.

Canaanite Cave in Bethlehem

Bethlehem was mentioned around 1350 B.C. in the *Tell al-Amarna* letters, from the **Egyptian** governor of Palestine to *Amenhotep III*. It was depicted as an important staging and rest stop for travelers from Syria and Palestine going to Egypt. The letters also signify that it was a boundary city of mid-Palestine and an outpost

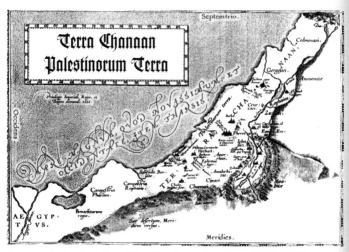

A map of the Holy Land by Abraham Ortelius (1527–1598)

looking out towards the desert. The Philistines had a garrison stationed in Bethlehem because it was a strong strategic point. They entered the land of the Canaanites, mingled with its people and settled in the southern coasts between Jaffa and Gaza. The **Philistines** had achieved a military supremacy over the greater part of the country around 1200 B.C, and called it Palestine.

The name of Bethlehem itself suggests a pastoral and agricultural life. The tale of Ruth,

King David, Sculpture by Angelo

Ruth gleaning in the field

the Moabite, and Boaz suggests an atmosphere of idyllic rusticity that is still obvious today. Ruth's grandson was King David of whose lineage Christ was born. A disagreement about the land between the Philistines and **Israeli** tribes caused numerous wars. David, who was born in Bethlehem, was driven with his tribe to the hills in the wilderness, where their adventures became the theme of various epic tales. One of these tales contains an allusion to the topography of Bethlehem: *"One summer's day David longed, and said, Oh that one would give me drink of the water of the well of Bethlehem,*

which is by the gate! And three mighty men break through the host of the Philistines, and draw water out of the well of Bethlehem, that was by the gate, and took it, and brought it to David: neverthe-less he would not drink thereof, but poured it out unto the lord". (2 Samuel 23, 14-16).

The narrative of the Old Testament mentions Bethlehem in the first book of the Bible when Jacob, son of Abraham, and his family were journeying to the city of Hebron passing by Bethlehem (Genesis 35:16). There, his wife Rachel died giving birth to Benjamin, and he buried her by the side of the

David's Well in Bethlehem

Bethlehem Road where her tomb has been a shrine to this day. In that time, Bethlehem was a small walled town erected on a hill in the northern part of the present town of Bethlehem as suggested by the reference in the story of David's well.

Greeks occupied Palestine for more than a century and remained until the arrival of the **Romans** in 160 B.C. The story of the town through this period is singularly and happily uneventful. The reason for this is partly geographical. The town lies just off the great road that in antiquity carried merchandise and travelers to and from Syria

Rachel Tomb, Bethlehem

and the Red Sea. A decree of Caesar Augustus, which commanded the taking of a census in all the provinces of the Roman Empire, brought Mary and Joseph to Bethlehem, thus fulfilling the prophecy of Micah, spoken 750 years before. When Jesus was born in Bethlehem, Herod the Great was a vassal of Rome and in 6 A.D. Palestine was included in the imperial province of Syria. The construction of Herod's palace, Herodium, in the 1st century B.C. must have brought the path through Bethlehem into more frequent use. St. Luke's mention of an inn at Bethlehem during Herod's reign fits well

The Slaughter of the Innocents

enough in the picture. There was also the dramatic slaughter of the Innocents by Herod who earlier instructed the Magi to report where the Baby Jesus was to be found. However, when he realized that he had been deceived by the Wise Men, he became furious and ordered the massacre of all the boys two years old and under in Bethlehem and its environs. *(Mtt. 2.16).* Emperor Hadrian in 135 A.D. profaned the sanctity of the Grotto of the Nativity and turned it into a pagan sanctuary. He had a grove of trees, dedicated to *Thammuz-Adonis*, planted over the Nativity grotto in the same way he had built temples to Venus and Jove in

Emperor Hardian

Jerusalem on mount Calvary and at the Sepulcher. The worship of Adonis, the personified spirit of the ripening, falling and regerminating grain, had been popular among the agricultural community. The festival of Adonis occurred once a year in the spring or summer.

From Hadrian's time until the reign of Constantine, the population worshipped Adonis in the cave where the infant Jesus was born. Palestine, consequently,

Emperor Constantine

was officially pagan as was the whole Roman empire until 313 when Constantine proclaimed Christianity as the religion of the state. In the year 325 the Bishop of Jerusalem, St. Marcarius, took the opportunity of acquainting the Emperor Constantine with the neglected condition of the Holy Places in his diocese. The Emperor ordered the construction, at public expense, of monumental churches to commemorate the three principal events of Jesus' life: the Nativity, the Crucifixion and the Resurrection. One of these was a church enshrining the scene of the Nativity. Christian traditions were so clear and deeply rooted that there was no problem in localizing the correct place, and it was possible to begin working the following year. Among the trees, not far from the village, was a cave which the local people and their parents had known for generations to be the birthplace of Jesus Christ. The cave was made the center of a scheme for the church and work began that same year.

With not much more than its church and convents, Bethlehem was still a small village, though famous as a place of pilgrimage. A fifth century visitor described Bethlehem as *situated on the narrow ridge of a mountain, surrounded on all sides by valleys, the ridge of ground stretching from east to west for about a mile. The level*

A view of the town of Bethlehem

ground on the top of the ridge was enclosed by a low wall without towers overlooking the valleys from the brow of the hill. The houses straggled along the main axis of the town. The Church of the Nativity stood at the eastern extremity of the town, a lofty structure covering a kind of a natural half-cave, whose inner part is called the Manger of the Lord. The town has no natural water supply, a factor which restricted its growth in antiquity. Until the Romans brought water by a pipe from springs beyond Solomon's pools the city relied on its rainfall, stored in cisterns.

Toward the end of the 4th century, Bethlehem became a very important center of monastic life. In 384 A.D. St. Jerome arrived from Rome with a group of pious and learned pilgrims. He came to Bethlehem to continue his work in an atmosphere of monastic life. He devoted himself to the tremendous task with which Pope St. Damasus had entrusted him, namely to review all old Latin translations of the Bible and produce a new version, the Vulgate, based on original Hebrew and Greek texts.

Saint Jerome, (347-420 A.D.)

St. Paula and her daughter Eustochium (386 A.D.)

Two Roman ladies of noble origin, St. Paula and her daughter Eustochium, moved to Bethlehem in 386 to lead an ascetic life along with St. Jerome. They founded the earliest monastic community in Bethlehem which has lasted, with some interruption, to this day. Paula used her riches to build a hospice for pilgrims and two monasteries, one for St. Jerome and his followers, and the other for herself and the nuns. In Bethlehem, St. Jerome was revered as the spiritual father of all those who tried to live in humility. This brought many well known pilgrims and recruits from the east and west. St. Jerome died in 420 and Eusebius of Cremona, a disciple of the great biblicist, was elected superior of the monastery. Unfortunately, Eusebius died two years later and after him Western monastic life did not survive long in Bethlehem.

When the Roman empire was divided in 395 into two empires, eastern and western, Palestine was joined to **Byzantium**, the eastern part. In the following years the life of the Latin-

Bethlehem on the Madaba Map, 6ᵗʰ century

speaking communities of Bethlehem faded from view, eclipsed by the growth and more spectacular austerities of an eastern monasticism. As a result, the town of Bethlehem prospered and its population increased with the spread of churches, monasteries, and convents in Bethlehem itself, and the surrounding areas. These included monks and hermits from different nationalities: Byzantine Greeks, Romans, Prussians, Armenians, Syriacs, Copts and others. During this period, the town was fortified and the walls strengthened by adding two towers; the town is represented in this way on the famous mosaic of Madaba: the most ancient map we know of depicting the Holy Land and its surroundings as they were known in the middle of the sixth century. The map was discovered in the town of Madaba in Jordan in 1884 on the floor of a Byzantine church ruins. In Bethlehem on the Madaba map we can see two towers and a large structure with a red dome. This is the Church of the Nativity.

In 527 A.D. Justinian became Emperor in Constantinople. Under his reign Palestine witnessed a time of prosperity and expansion for its churches and for monasticism. Afterwards, in

Emperor Justinian (527 A.D.)

529, the Samaritans rebelled against the Byzantine state and overran the country, plundering and destroying as they went. Churches and monasteries, towns and villages were all pillaged or gutted by fire. The walls of Bethlehem and its main church were destroyed. The revolt was soon quelled. At the same time the church was rebuilt in a grand style, the town wall and the defenses of the

Caliph 'Umar (637 A.D.)

monasteries were repaired. Other monasteries were probably built at this time, and there are now in or near Bethlehem at least four monasteries besides those of St. Paula and St. Jerome.

A few years later (614) the country was invaded by the **Persians**. According to an oral tradition, they did not cause any damage to the Church of the Nativity because they saw the picture of the three Magi dressed as Persians, carrying gifts to Christ at his birth. Outside and above the roof of the narthex, the gable end overlooking the atrium was decorated with a

The Persians (614 A.D.)

mosaic scene of the birth of Christ with his mother holding the Child to her breast. On their arrival at Bethlehem the Persians were amazed at the picture which included the adoration of the Persian Magi. In respect and affection for their ancestors, whom they venerated as if they were alive, they spared the church.

In 637, soon after his entry into Jerusalem, the **Muslim** Caliph *'Umar ibn al-Khattab* visited Bethlehem and performed his devotions before the southern apse of the basilica. The relations between 'Umar and the ecclesiastical authorities were friendly and a written agreement was granted to the Patriarch Sofronious that Muslims would pray in the church as individuals only, without assembly or *muezzin*. A covenant known as *'Umar's Covenant* was issued and handed to the Patriarch.

Christians and Muslims lived together in a peaceful manner. Muslims had the right to pray in the southern apse, conveniently oriented towards Mecca, and

The Covenant of 'Umar

This is a Covenant from me, 'Umar ibn al-Khattab, given on the Mount of Olives in the District of al-Quds ash-Sharif (noble Jerusalem) to the venerable father Sofronius, Patriarch of the Malakite people including all Christian congregations, priests, monks and nuns, wherever they are, and wherever in the future they may be found. Let them be safeguarded because free non Muslim subjects who observe the rules of Ahl-Dhimmah must enjoy our protection, and be granted full safety by us believers and all those who succeed us.

Let this safety be guaranteed to their persons, their churches, monasteries and all their holy sites, inside and out including: the Holy Sepulcher in Jerusalem, Bethlehem, the birth place of Jesus (Peace be upon him), its large church and its grotto with the three doors facing east, north and west. We hereby also grant safety to all remaining Christian denominations that are present here and those that come on pilgrimage and visits from Franks, Copts, Syrians, Armenians, Nestorians, Jacobites and Maronites – all followers of the afore – mentioned Patriarch who shall be their superior. This guarantee of safety is granted in deference to our beloved Prophet who was sent by God and who honored these people by the stamp of his noble hand (referring to the Covenant given by the Prophet to the monks of Tur Sinai) ordering that they be safeguarded and protected. Accordingly, we believers are treating them well in honor of the one who treated them well. We shall be exempt from poll taxes and all their obligations: they shall be safe from all afflictions and tribulations on land or at sea. They shall be allowed to enter and leave their Holy Sepulcher and all their other holy places freely and without hindrance of charges.

Christians cared for the building maintenance. This common cultic life should not be surprising. Muslims respect Christ as a prophet and venerate Our Lady. The tolerant policy was maintained by Umar's successors till 1009. In that year a fanatic Caliph, al-Hakim, the one who had destroyed the Holy Sepulcher, declared a real persecution against Christians. Bethlehem was once more spared because al-Hakim wished to continue receiving the tribute Christians had been paying since Umar's day.

The conquest of Palestine by the **Crusaders** in the year 1099 began a new chapter in the history of Bethlehem. Within a short time the Franks (Crusaders) took over from the local clergy and installed a community of Augustinian canons (the first religious order of men in the Roman Catholic Church) under a prior who conducted services in the Latin language. The former clergy remained to minister to the local congregation and to pilgrims from the eastern parts of Christendom. On Christmas Day, 1101 Bald-

The Crusadors near Bethlehem

win, the first king of the Latin Kingdom, was crowned by the Patriarch in Bethlehem, avoiding thereby the scandal of receiving a temporal crown in the city where Christ was crowned with thorns. His successor Baldwin II, and his queen followed this example in 1122.

The Crusaders reconstructed the town and made it a fortified outpost. They remained for about two centuries during which the town of Bethlehem prospered. Some of them intermarried with the local people and settled down. The 12th century opened Bethlehem to European social and ecclesiastical influences to an extent which had not been possible before. From every country, pilgrims could now visit the Holy Places bringing with them offerings to the church and prosperity to the merchants whose shops were built in front of it. In 1100, the Crusader King Baldwin succeeded in having Pope Pascal II establish a bishopric in Bethlehem.

During the Crusaders period, the restoration of the Church of the Nativity took place between the years 1165 and 1169. Old and worn out floor-marbles were replaced; the new roof of cedar wood was covered with lead; side walls disappeared under white marble slabs; the upper part of the nave glittered with mosaics; and the vault in the Nativity grotto was embellished with multicolored mosaics, either composed of glass or mother-of-pearl cubes. The church itself was encompassed

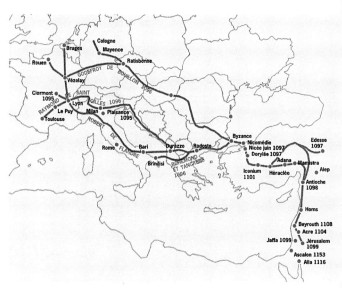

The first crusaders (1095-1099)

The Nativity Church: prespective drawing by Bernardino Amico 1595

with a high wall and towers which gave it the strength and appearance of an independent fortress.

In 1187, **Saladin** the Ayyubite captured Bethlehem. Although the Church of the Nativity came to no harm, the relations with the West were abruptly cut off, and the Latin (Catholic) Bishop and Canons were forced to leave. The life of the local people was seriously affected by the expulsion of the Latin community and the temporary interruption of the stream of western pilgrims on which the Bethlehemites primarily depended. However, because two treaties, one signed by emperor Frederick II and Malek el-Kamel, sultan of Egypt, and the second by the King of Navarre and the Sultan of Damascus, Bethlehem was in Christian hands from 1229 to 1244. The Canons of St. Augustine could return to their convent and the Basilica was once more opened to the Christian world.

In 1250, the Ayyubid Dynasty was replaced in Egypt by Circassian **Mamlukes**, and the accession of the fanatical Sultan Rukn ed-Din Beibars brought an end to the tradition of tolerance that helped safeguard the Holy places. In 1263, Beibars ordered the dismantling of the towers and walls of Bethlehem. The church itself was not damaged but Christians were banished from Bethlehem.

In the following century, western influences were reinforced; monks from the order of

The Gate of Bethlehem.
Painting by George Samour

the Franciscan Friars Minor were established in Bethlehem in the old Augustinian priory, where they still reside. The Franciscan Fathers had acquired possession of the grotto in 1347 and also, the right to administer the Basilica and to care for its maintenance. The Franciscan Custos, Giovanni, obtained from the sultan Qaita Bey consent to renovate the roof of the Church of the Nativity. A few years later European influences at Bethlehem were setback by the expulsion of the Catholic Latin clergy for the second time.

With the **Turkish** occupation in 1517, the period of conflict between the Franciscans and the Greeks for the possession of the Sanctuaries began. Consequently, the Basilica passed from the Franciscans to the Greeks according to the favor enjoyed at the Sublime Porte (Ottoman Caliph) by the nation which supported the communities (Catholics or Orthodox). Under the Turkish regime the question of ownership and rights in the Holy places took on an increasingly political and even international dimension. The first question in the dispute between France and Russia was concerned with the possession of the keys to the main doors of the Basilica. The second was concerned with the mysterious removal, one night in the year 1747, of a silver star bearing a Latin inscription, which was put into a slab of marble beneath the altar of the Nativity. In 1740, a treaty was concluded between France and Turkey, wherein France was given the right to protect the Christians of

Bethlehem. Painting by David Roberts (1839)

Time Line Map
From Canaanites to the Palestinians

3000 B.C.	Canaanite civilization	629	Byzantine domination
1200 B.C.	Philistine period	637	Islamic conquest
1000 B.C.	Hebrew period	1099–1187	The Crusaders
587 B.C.	Assyrian domination	1187–1250	Ayyubite period
533 B.C.	Egyptian domination	1250–1516	Mameluke period
332 B.C.	Greek domination	1515–1917	Othoman period
313 A.D.	The Roman Empire is converted to Christianity	1922–1948	British Mandate
		1948–1967	Jordanian period
614 A.D.	Persian domination	1967–1995	Israeli occupation
		1995	The Palestinian Authority

Bethlehem in the 19th century

the East. Thus in 1852, the Catholics were allowed to place a silver star in the place where Christ was born. Also, the *firman* of the Sultan *Abdul Mejid* contained a guarantee for the Status Quo in the Sanctuaries. In 1853, Russia declared war against Turkey (the Crimean War) to retain its right to protect the Christians and their Holy places. Between 1810 and 1829 the Armenians succeeded in establishing themselves in the Church, getting the left arm of the transept.

During the Turkish period, looting became open and undisguised; marble was removed from the walls of the Church of the Nativity and Bethlehem suffered from bitter and bloody struggles between the Catholics and Orthodox for hegemony in the Nativity church. However, between the 17th and 18th centuries Bethlehem was on the verge of modern times. Long and continuous contact by the local people with travelers from western Christendom had familiarized them with the manners and tastes of western countries, and improved their economic condition. The sale of Olive Wood and Mother-of-Pearl had become the means of livelihood for a substantial section of the population.

The Nativity Star

A man from Bethlehem

A woman from Bethlehem

The country was in Egyptian hands for ten years beginning in 1831. However, during this period, robbery and violence were too common, and the murder of a favorite of Ibrahim Pasha in 1834, resulted in the destruction of the Muslim quarter of the town and the disarming of the whole population. By 1841 Bethlehem was again in Turkish hands. The result was unemployment, oppression, compulsory military service and heavy taxes imposed on the inhabitants. This oppressive situation forced the people of Bethlehem to emigrate abroad, especially to the Americas, to earn a living and improve their life-style. A great number of Bethlehemites emigrated to foreign countries especially to Latin America and Europe. By the end of the 19th century, some

Portrait of a Bethlehem Family

of the sons of the trading families settled abroad, carrying out the responsibility of the diffusion of religious articles, the only industry in Bethlehem at that time. At the same time, several European missionaries came to Bethlehem and built schools.

The Balfour Declaration was issued by Great Britain in 1917 giving the Jews the right to a national home in Palestine provided that the rights of the original people of the country were respected. In 1918, Palestine was placed under the British Mandate. Wars between the Arabs and Jews continued and the latter occupied most of Palestine and declared their state 'Israel'. The town of Bethlehem remained unoccupied and towards the end of 1948, the union of the eastern part of Palestine and Trans-Jordan was declared under the name of the Hashemite Kingdom of Jordan.

A second war between the Arabs and Israelis broke out in 1967, and the latter occupied the remainder of Palestine including Bethlehem. The Palestinian *Intifada* or popular uprising against the Israeli occupation of the West Bank and Gaza Strip began on December 8, 1987 with the ultimate goal, the establishment of an independent Palestinian state under the leadership of the PLO, to be arrived at through negotiation in an international peace conference. Bethlehem remained under the Israeli occupation until December 22, 1995 when the Palestinian Authority took over in compliance with the Oslo Accord of 1993. The process of peace and reconciliation in the Middle East is openning a new era in Bethlehem's long history. Economically, the peace process is creating numerous opportunities for investors and new industries. Tourism in particular is likely to develop into an even more important mainstay of the local economy, for the dawn of the new Millenium is bound to draw large numbers of visitors to this historic city.

The signing ceremony of the Oslo Accord, 1993

Bethlehem Today

Bethlehem today: General view

The town of Bethlehem, known all over the world as the place where Jesus Christ was born, is today more of a bustling tourist resort than the holy place you would expect. It is full of tourists, and souvenir shops, restaurants and bars which are part of the services that mark the city. Bethlehem and its satellite towns, *Beit Sahour* and *Beit Jala* have many churches, convents, schools and hospitals. The Greek Orthodox have 15 churches and institutions. The Roman Catholics have 25. There are 8 Protestant churches. The Syriac Orthodox have one church and the Greek Catholics have two churches. The Ethiopians and the Copts have one each. There are also a number of Mosques; the most important one is the *Mosque of 'Umar* across the square from the Church of the Nativity. This mosque was established in 1849.

You will find numerous foreign institutions in the district; some are of a religious nature, and others are not. Among them are the Holy Family Hospital that belongs to the Knights of Malta, The Christian Society for the Holy Land Hospital, Efeta Institution for the Deaf and Dumb, The Children's Village S.O.S, Caritas Children's Hospital, Sira (a Swedish Institute for the Handicapped), the Salisians Technical School and many others.

Location:

Modern Bethlehem is an agricultural market and trade center closely linked to nearby Jerusalem. It lies at a distance of 10 kms (6 miles) to the south of the Old City of Jerusalem. It is situated on a mountainous site, 777 meters (2600 feet) above the level of the Mediterranean Sea and overlooks its surroundings. Its surface resembles the shape of a semi circle. From the west, the town of Bethlehem is bounded by the town of Beit Jala and from the east by the town of Beit Sahour. From the north it is bordered by Jerusalem and the village of Sur Bahir and from the south by Solomon's Pools and the villages of al-Khader and Artas. Forty thousand live in the administrative limits of the municipality of Bethlehem and five thousand in the old center of the town. As a symbol of the increased intermingling of the region's people, beside Arabic, the native language, English is widely spoken. French, German and Spanish are spoken too.

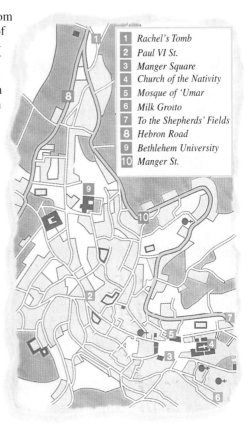

1	Rachel's Tomb
2	Paul VI St.
3	Manger Square
4	Church of the Nativity
5	Mosque of 'Umar
6	Milk Grotto
7	To the Shepherds' Fields
8	Hebron Road
9	Bethlehem University
10	Manger St.

Plan of Bethlehem

Leaving Jerusalem towards Bethlehem, you will find yourself on the Hebron-Bethlehem road. At the main entrance, on the right, the shrine of Rachel's Tomb, Prophet Jacob's wife, is located. The road then splits

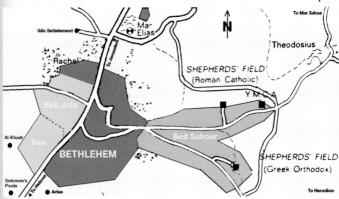

Plan for Bethlehem and its District

into two branches which run correspondent to each other: Manger Street and the Hebron Road.

Manger Street:

The Manger Street on the left, leads to the town center, the Manger Square and the Church of the Nativity. All along Manger Street, are numerous large souvenir shops in which you find various kinds of artistic crafts such as mother-of-pearl and olive wood, as well as embroidery, religious post cards and others, along with leather, silver, brass, golden items, diamonds and jewelry. You will also see various kinds of restaurants, cafes and bars.

Going up Manger Street from Manger Square to Rachel's Tomb, you see the following places: After leaving Manger Square, there is a road to the right leading to the town of Beit-Sahour and the Shepherds'

Fields. St. Joseph's Secondary School for girls is on the left. The next road on the right leads to the S.O.S village. Farther along the road is the Syriac Catholic church and Saint Joseph's Home. As you round the corner on the left side of the road is the American Christian Mission with a hospital. Going up Manger Street you pass through the shopping area. After leaving the shopping area another road on the right leads to the S.O.S Village and another road on the left goes up the hill to *al-Azah* refugee camp and Bethlehem University. Farther over, on the right (200 meters before the end of the street) a

Syriac Catholic Church and Saint Joseph's Home

road on the left leads to the Antonian Home for Aged Women run by the Sisters of Artas; next you will see the First Baptist Church and Mar Andrea (*Bethlehem University Residence*). Farther over on the hillside is the Caritas Baby Hospital

St. Joseph School

Caritas Baby Hospital

Dar Jasir

run by the sisters of the Holy Cross of Mentzingen. Passing the Caritas Hospital we find a road on the left that leads to the monastery of the Emmanuel Sisters. Going back to Manger St. you find the Paradise Hotel at right and al-'Azah refugee camp on the left. The next road on the right before the end of Manger St. is Caritas St. and leads to the Applied Research Institute.

Hebron Road:

The Hebron Road on the right branch of the fork mentioned above, nearly separates the boundaries of the town of Bethlehem and Beit-Jala and leads to the town suburbs. Following the Hebron road from Rachel's Tomb to the south, you find on the right a Secondary School for girls in *Dar Jacir* one of the most beautiful buildings of Bethlehem. Shortly

Bethlehem Bible College

after, there is the Bethlehem Bible College and exactly at the cross roads, the House of St. Teresa (a university residence for girls). The road on the left leads to the higher part of town and to Bethlehem University, and the one on the right leads to the Governate of Bethlehem and to Beit-Jala. Following the Hebron road, on the right hand is the House of Hope for the Blind and the Mentally handicapped, and on the left is the Jerusalem Open University. On the left hand corner of the crossroad is the Institute for Deaf and Dumb run by the Sisters of St. Dorothea. This crossroads is known as *Bab-Izqaq (Gate of the Alleys)*. To the left, Paul VI St. leads to the center of the town of Bethlehem and as-Sahel St. to the right leads directly to the town of Beit-Jala. Hebron road passes by Bethlehem District Military Headquarter, Dehesheh refugee camp, al-Khader village, Solomon's Pools and leads to the city of Hebron at a distance of 25 kms (15.5 miles).

The *Dehesheh* refugee camp was established in 1949, after the war of 1948 which led to the

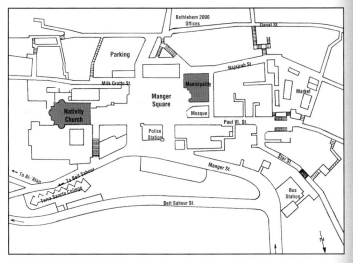

Map of the Manger Square

flight of many Palestinians from their homeland. Its population is estimated to be 9000.

The length of Bethlehem in the direction of Hebron Road between Rachel's Tomb and Dehesheh region is 3 kms (1.8 miles), and its breadth between the borders of Beit-Jala and Beit Sahour is 2 kms (1.2 miles). Its area within the Municipality borders is about eight square kilometers.

Manger Square:

Manger Square is the town's central area. At present, it is used as a bus and car parking lot. On the Eastern part of the Manger Square, you can see the *Armenian Convent*. Behind it,

Bethlehem Municipality

there is the Milk Grotto Street with its numerous souvenir shops that sell mainly hand made crafts: crucifixes, medals, rosaries, figurines and boxes carved in olive wood and mo-

The Spring (al-'Ain)

ther-of-pearl, and silver jewelry. The work is done in small workshops and executed in mother-of-pearl and olive wood. This has been the chief industry of Bethlehem for several centuries. To the right of the Milk Grotto Street, a steep road leads down to the *Qawawsah* Quarter, to al-'Ain (*the spring*)

Mosque of 'Umar

which was the town's water reservoir, to *Bethlehem 2000 Steering Committee* offices and to Mar Shar-bel Convent on Qanah Street.

An arched building of three floors stretches along the southern side of the square. Mainly souvenir shops occupy the ground floor and the Ministry of Tourism the second floor; other offices and a small hotel are in the upper floors. On the western side you see the Bethlehem Municipality built in 1975. The post office occupies the lower floor, the Cairo-Amman Bank, and St. George Restaurant occupy the ground floor. You also see the lofty minaret of the mosque of 'Umar, rebuilt in 1954. The mosque of Bethlehem has become too small to accommodate the numerous faithful of the city, who spread out during Friday prayers among the cars parked in the Square. Between the two buildings is a road that leads to the *Najajrah*

Quarter and the Municipal Market, then to the *Fawaghrah* Quarter and *al-Madbassah* Square. Beside, to the right of the Mosque there is Paul VI street. On the northern side is a police station.

Paul VI Street:

As souvenir of the pilgrimage of Paul VI, the first Pope who came to Bethlehem, the main trading street which crosses the town from the east to the west, from the Manger Square to the crossroad *Bab-iz-qaq* was given his name. On entering the street at a distance of a few meters from the Mosque, you will find a museum of traditional clothes and heritage items, belonging to the

Paul VI. Street

Arab Women's Union, called *Our Old Bethlehem Home*. As you head out from the Museum, the Star Square will be very close. On going up the stairs from Star Square you will find the Market *(Souq)* on your left and the *Syriac Orthodox Church* on the right. This market was once in the Manger Square, and used to attract a lot of peasants and Bedouins from

Market Place and Syriac Or-thodox Church

Holy Family Church

all around the region, but in 1929 it was transferred to this place. At the end of the stairs, the street narrows to three meters wide (10 feet), and continues until it reaches an intersection, where one will find al-Fawaghrah Quarter on the left, and to the right a street leading to the *Salesian's Convent*. On going up 50 meters (150 feet), you find on the next intersection the Lutheran Church on your left, and the Salesian Technical School on your right. Continuing on your walk, you will pass al-Madbassah square then al-Bandak's building housing the Grand Hotel. At that point another street intersects Paul VI St. leading to Star Hotel, St. Joseph's Nuns' Convent and girls' school, and to Bethlehem University. If you continue your walk in the main street, you reach another intersection known as Cinema Square. On the right, a one way road leads to the Arab Women's Union Society. On the left, Nasser street leads to the Shepherd Hotel, the Monastery of Betharram Fathers, The Carmelite Sisters' Convent, *College des Frères* and the new Rosary Sisters' Convent. Walking down Paul VI street, on your right is the Holy Family Hospital and church run by the Sisters of Charity. Beside the Hospital there is a *Créche*, which usually has some 90-100 orphans and straight ahead you reach the cross-road known as *bab-iz-qaq*. Walking through Paul VI street is enjoyable for visitors and shoppers of all tastes for they can find a variety of items.

Salesian's Convent

Qaus Az-Zararah

Stairway to Salesian Convent

Star Street:

Star Street begins at Star Square, two minutes away from Manger Square, and continues to the site of the Wells of David. Leaving Star Square, you turn to the right through the old town and continue through *Qaus Az-Zararah,* known as the oldest principal gate to the town. Below you on the right is St. Joseph Secondary School for girls

Greek Catholic Church

(1883). On the left there is the Greek Catholic Church. The stairway leads up to the Salesian Convent. Continuing on, you pass on the left the Convent of the Rosary Sisters, founded in 1893. This part of town is called *Ras Efteis.* A road on the right leads into the Catholic Action Club and the Wells of David. Below, on the Manger Street the Church and school of the Syriac Catholics now run by the Dominican Sisters of Catherine of Siena. On the left the road leads to the shopping area of Manger Street.

Al-Madbassah Square:

Al-Madbassah Square in the Old City of Bethlehem is near the Lutheran Church and in front of the Salisian convent. The Square lies on top of a hill, which constitutes the western gate or entrance to the old city of Bethlehem. In the old days the square was the site of a molasses mill, where Bethlehemites came to make *dibis* (molasses) out of their grape harvest. Hence, the square took the name al-Madbassah or the molasses mill. The square with its surrounding area is part of a regular route for tourists to take when visiting Bethlehem. The square provides a central location from which one can reach Bethlehem and its surrounding areas easily, quickly and cheaply. There is a taxi station that connects Beit Jala, Artas, Solomon's Pools and al-Khader. The square is surrounded by a colorful shopping street where the pulse of Arabic life can be experienced first hand. The square, like the rest of the old city of Bethlehem today, suffers from dilapidation and insufficient infrastructure networks and traffic jams. Once renovated, the square will become an attractive location to visit.

The Old Center:

If one scans Bethlehem's horizon, there is an unusual array of towers and belfries, domes and spires, houses of worship of all kinds, red-tiled roofs of monasteries and convents. Along its steep streets and lanes flows the daily life; the market place,

The Old Center

Traditional Architecture

the little retail shops, the children pouring out of school, and the cafes where the men haggle and gossip over little cups of Arabic coffee. The narrow Bethlehem roads were paved with stone. Some were topped by rocky arches supported by the house walls from two sides, bearing houses and windows which give you a charming idea about the art of architecture in those days. It cannot be denied that the impressions left with visitors when touring the old city with its unique architectural styles and the strong oriental presence, will never be forgotten.

UNESCO has worked together with the Municipality of Bethlehem to assemble the elements for a plan of preservation and enhancement of the old center of the town, to recover its old charm, restore its architectural pattern, and save the Palestinian cultural heritage of this historic town on the eve of the

twenty first century. The project is intended, in particular, to rehabilitate certain public areas of the old town center. Unesco took the initiative to organize a roving photographic exhibition "Bethlehem 2000" which offers a compendium of 80 images of today's Bethlehem to raise the awareness of the public and donors.

The Architectural Style:

The traditional architectural style of the old center of Bethlehem gives a medieval aspect to the town with its narrow streets and arches. *Old Houses* were simple in shape and built with white stone called *Mizzi hilu* "sour sweet". Their external and internal walls, ceilings in the shape of an arch, floor tiles, roof and stairs were also built of the same white stone. The breadth of the external walls was about one and a quarter meters (4 feet), and the internal was about eighty centimeters

Local Architectural Style

(2.8 feet). Due to war and fear of enemy raids, it was later necessary for houses to be built adjacent to one another, and on top of one another, some four stories high. This facilitated co-operation between residents in the defense of their homes and protection against enemy attacks. The buildings took the shape of a complex and their external appearance resembled that of a fortress. The ground floor rarely had any windows, but on the upper stories ordinary single or double windows were built with their tops frequently constructed in the shape of an arch. Due to the slope of most building sites, part of the building consisted of a basement topped by a ground floor over the entire area. The base-

Local Architectural Style

ment was normally used to shelter animals. *Thus, it is possible that St. Joseph might have stayed with Mary in such a house: the Virgin would have thus given birth to Jesus in the basement.* The Arab Women's Union in Bethlehem established a museum representing such an ancient Bethlehem house. You will find it close to Manger Square (2 minutes walk only).

Pre-Modern Buildings were built towards the end of the Ottoman rule (1516-1916), through

Basement of an old house

the advent of missions and the construction of institutions, convents, churches, hospitals and the like and through the return of certain emigrants. The sons of Bethlehem are great travellers and traders. They have emigrated to many countries and especially to South America. There they have prospered and from thence they have sent back much wealth, with which the grand mansions constructed mostly of a hard red stone trimmed with a soften white one, have been built. They built palaces resembling the palaces

The Hermas Building (Bethlehem University)

of Europe, such as the palace of *Sulaiman Jacir* built in 1910 and the palace of *Abu Hermas*, *Handal* and *Jaqaman*. This beautiful building, known as *Hermas* (1910), is adjacent to the campus of Bethlehem University. It was purchased and totally renovated to offer all the advantages of a modern facility in a traditional setting. It houses the Faculties of Nursing and Education.

Modern buildings started to be built during the British rule (1920-1948) after the end of the First World War. An influx of emigrants returned from the diaspora with great eagerness to settle in Bethlehem, building new homes to reside in. The art of architecture developed by using cement and iron in the shape of thin bars. It then became necessary to plan for the growth of the town, so one of the laws of the Municipality was that all the façades of the buildings must be built with stone, even though they might vary in kind and color. For the last few years, there has been an intensive wave of building construction on the hill slopes that rise in terraces. Most of the expansion, has been at the expense of the historical center and the succession of vine, olive, almond and fig clad terraces to the valleys which surround it on every side. Many trees have been cut and several roads were constructed, and as a response to population pressure, the Bethlehem Municipality recently began granting permits for buildings exceeding the previous limit of three stories.

Churches & Religious Institutions:

Right in the middle of Bethlehem's cluster of white houses, rise the bell towers of numerous religious institutions like shepherds watching over their flocks. French and Italian Catholic institutions were the pioneers, followed by the Protestant societies.

Betharam Convent, Daher Mountain and Dehesheh Camp

The Franciscans (1347) have a large convent within the parish church of St. Catherine, two parish schools: Terra Santa School for Boys and a girls' school, conducted by the Sisters of St. Joseph, and a pilgrim hospice (Casa Nova).

The French Convent of the Carmelite Sisters (1888), built after the fashion of the Castle of Saint Angelo at Rome, lies in the south-west quarter of the town; adjoining this is a church, and the convent of the Fathers of the Sacred Heart of Betharam, built in 1878. From 1920 to 1948, it became the clerical school for the seminarists of the congregation. It is now a center adapted for groups of priests, men and women, religious and lay-people wishing to find a place of quiet in a prayerful atmosphere in the Holy Land. It is also open to those who organize sessions for biblical or spiritual renewal. The house has about thirty single rooms with all modern comforts and it is ten minutes walk from the Grotto of the Nativity.

The Italian Salisians, who came in 1863, have rendered invaluable service in training generations of skilled professionals. On a hill side, in the northern part of Bethlehem, the Salisians occupy a cluster between the Salesian Street, Paul VI Street and *El-Batin* Street; it includes two convents, a church, an orphanage and a technical school. These buildings were constructed between 1863 and 1905, under the auspices of Father Don Belloni, attached to which is the Chapel of Saint Louis. Their technical school, with its many branches, has become the pride of Bethlehem. On Paul VI Street near the Hebron Road, lies the Holy Family Church and Hospital (1889) run by the Knights of Malta and a crèche run by the Sisters of Charity.

The Franciscan Missionaries of Mary known as *The White Sisters* have a Convent (1906)

The White Sisters Convent

by Father Ernest Schnydrig and supported by the members of *Caritas Kinderhilfe Bethlehem;* this hospital is run by the Sisters of the Holy Cross of Menzingen (Switzerland).

The Swedes have their twin

Bethlehem University Chapel

near the Milk Grotto. The Convent hosted young orphan girls and the first kindergarten in Bethlehem. It now hosts a Family Care Center and a hostel.

The Rosary Sisters have an elementary school on Star Street, a new convent, a novice and a kindergarten on Nasser St.

The Brothers of the Christian Schools occupied since 1893 the summit of the western hill, where they have leading educational institutions: Bethlehem University and the Fréres Secondary School on Nasser St.

Caritas Children's Hospital on Caritas Street is the only specialized pediatric clinic in the West Bank with a ward for intensive care and premature babies. It was founded in 1952

institutions for retarded children in Bethlehem. The Germans run S.O.S. Children's Village, accommodating abandoned children and orphans.

The House of Hope for the Blind and Mentally Handicapped on Hebron Road is financed

Bethlehem University: Faculty of Arts.

by Christians from the U.K. The Antonian Charitable Society, founded in 1913 by a young Palestinian, looks after helpless old women and aged widows who are in dire need of vital human care and love. It runs a nursery and an out-patient clinic, and operates one of the best houses for elderly women on the West Bank. It is known as the Antonian Home for the Aged. The Sisters of Dorothea run *Epheta*, an institute for the deaf and blind founded in 1964 after the visit of Pope Paul VI to the Holy Land. The Terresian Association founded the Home of St. Terresa; a university residence for girls and runs the Pontifical Mission Library (1972): a community library which provides an extensive collection of books and periodicals.

There is a Coptic Orthodox Chapel since 1988 on the Milk Grotto Street. A Maronite Convent and Mar Sharbel House are on Qanah Street. There is a Greek Catholic Church on Star Street. There is also a sizable Arab Orthodox congregation and an equally large Roman Catholic community.

Through missionary and educational activities in the last century, Protestant churches began to have followers and convents; today one finds many members of the Anglican and Lutheran churches. However, the first Lutheran church and school was erected in 1854. The church with the spire on the western side of the town was built by Ludwing Schneller with the help of Empress Augusta Victoria who obtained in 1886, from the Othoman

The Lutheran Nativity Church

authorities a permit to build the church. Welhelm II, the German Emperor, visited the church in 1898. Today the church is attached to a co-educational secondary school, the International Center of Bethlehem *(Dar An-Nadwa)* and a hostel (Jubran House).

Prayers in Bethlehem may be said in all conceivable Eastern and Western tongues. It would be hard to enumerate all the chapels large and small in the town, but it seems that every shade of Christianity maintains institutions here in its own tongue *(see the List of Churches)*. Furthermore, there is a continual mushrooming of religious and charitable institutions.

Christmas in Bethlehem:

The year's highlight in Bethlehem is Christmas. There are actually three celebrations: the Western observance occurs on December 25, according to the Gregorian calendar; the Ortho-

Christmas Celebrations in the Manger Square

dox is celebrated on January 6, according to the older Julian calendar; and finally the Armenian on January 19. On these days, the town is festive with lights and banners, and the churches are full of worshippers and visitors. Carols pour from loud-speakers in the crowded Manger Square, and brisk trade is done in the carved olive wood and mother-of-pearl souvenirs for which Bethlehem is renowned.

Among the exciting aspects of Bethlehem's Christmas are the parades of Palestinian scouts through the town of Bethlehem. They mass in Manger Square to greet each Patriarch on his arrival from Jerusalem. Some scout processions start from Rachel's tomb and march to Manger Square, through Star Street. This is the route which is followed every Christmas Eve by the clergy of Jerusalem, led by the Patriarch, as they march in a solemn procession to the historic

Local Clergy waiting for the Arrival of the Patriarch

Church of Nativity. As they proceed to Manger Square, they are met by local clergy of Bethlehem. Troops from various sectarian groupings march together in front of the Patriarchs' processions through the winding streets of town, with local people and foreign pilgrims, crowded together. Crowds of up to 100,000 visitors and tourists from around the world cram the square from the morning to watch the procession. When each Patriarch meets the dignitaries and then enters the church, the scouts disperse. The climax on Christmas eve for the Roman Catholics is the elaborate midnight Mass in the presence of dignitaries and diplomats. Other churches have their own special services in Bethlehem and Jerusalem. In the evening the crowds gather at the Manger Square to listen to various choirs and orchestras which sing Christmas carols. On Christmas day many people go to the Shepherds' Field Church in Beit Sahour to attend afternoon prayers in the old subterranean grotto and to watch the procession of local clergy to the Shepherds' Field Church joined by the Boys Scouts complete with bands.

Bethlehem 2000

The year 2000 is attracting great worldwide attention. Agencies and institutions all over the world are planning festivities to mark the turn of the millennium. The year 2000 has special meaning for the city of Bethlehem, the birth place of Jesus Christ. Over five million tou-

The Parade of Palestinian Scouts in Beit Sahour

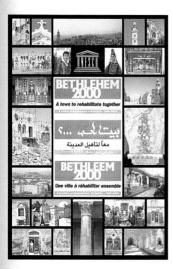

Photographic exhibition Bethlehem 2000

rists and pilgrims are expected to visit this holy town on this occasion. The city will be inviting high-ranking religious and political figures to join in the festivities. The new millennium will be celebrated in the city with a variety of concerts, festivals and other events.

In order to commemorate an event of such importance to all mankind, a pilot project, *Bethlehem 2000,* has been assembled. The project is a chance to highlight, through an urban policy, some of the issues of culture, tourism and economy which mark the re-birth of society, and thereby place a new milestone on the road to a culture of peace in the Middle East. The project covers different areas of the town which are vital to its development: rehabilitation of the street façades and squares of the old city, rehabilitation of the market place, redesign and construction of Nativity Square, identifying pedestrian zones, parking areas and construction of a bus station.

The Palestinian National Authority views the Bethlehem 2000 Project as a matter of major priority and urgency. It officially formed the International Committee for Bethlehem 2000, headed by President Yaser Arafat. On February 6th,

For more information

On action taken by **UNESCO** contact:

Coordination Unit for Assistance to the Palestinian People, UNESCO, 7 Place Fontenoy 75007 Paris, France.
Tel: 33/1 45681899
Fax: 33/1-45685675, Email: o.massalha@unesco.org
Internet:
http://www.unesco.org
Local office in Bethlehem: Tel: 742066, Fax: 742067 Qanah Street.

On action taken by the **Palestinian Authority**, contact:

Bethlehem 2000 Steering Committee, P.O.Box. 2000, Bethlehem. Tel: 742224, Fax: 742227
or
Bethlehem Municipality, P.O.Box. 48, Bethlehem. Tel: 972 2 741325, Fax: 741327

On action taken by **local groups** contact:

Dr. Qustandi Shomali, Bethlehem University, P.O.Box 9, Bethlehem. Telfax: 972 2 6473957. E-Mail: qshomali@bethlehem.edu.

1997. Dr. Hanan Ashrawi was appointed as Secretary General of this committee in order to formulate the broad policy and address the international dimention of this massive project.

KÖLN

STÄDTE-PARTNERSCHAFT

توأمة المدن

كولونيا

BETHLEHEM

بيت لحم

A twinning pact between Bethlehem and Cologne was signed in 1996

The Name of Bethlehem

The name of Bethlehem has been given to many cities in the world. The following list which is not comprehensive, shows the countries which gave the name of Bethlehem to one of their cities:

Bethlehem	Argentine
Bethlehem	Brazil (Para)
Bethlehem	Colombia
Bethlehem	Mexico
Bethlehem	Palestine
Bethlehem	Panama
Bethlehem	Paraguay
Bethlehem	Portugal
Bethlehem	South Africa
Bethlehem	Uruguay

U.S.A.:

Bethlehem	Pennsylvania
Bethlehem	Connecticut
Bethlehem	Georgia
Bethlehem	Indiana
Bethlehem	Kentucky
Bethlehem	Maryland
Bethlehem	New Hampshire
Bethlehem	South Dakota

Twinning with Bethlehem

The following cities have signed a twinning pact with Bethlehem:

Florence	Italy	1962
Abu Dabi	U.A.E.	1977
Athens	Greece	1987
Cordoba	Spain	1988
Assisi	Italy	1989
Glasgow	U. K.	1992
Burlington	U.S.A.	1993
Chartre	France	1994
Cosco	Peru	1994
Lisbon	Portugal	1995
Saint-Herblain	France	1995
Madaba	Jordan	1995
Cologne	Germany	1996
Orvitio	Italy	1996
Valenoz	Brazil	1996
Grometio	Italy	1996
Sarpsbourg	Norway	1997
Verona	Italy	1997
Chivita-vecchia	Italy	1997

Church of the Nativity

Nativity Church

The present Church of the Nativity is one of the earliest Christian structures. The original Basilica, erected in the 4th century by Emperor Constantine, was completely destroyed in the Samaritan Revolt of 529 A.D. It was replaced during the reign of Justinian (527-65) on the same site, by a larger Basilica, slightly different in plan and incorporating different parts of the original building. This Basilica was built in the shape of a cross with a tripartite apse. The atrium was transformed into a narthex, and two flights of stairs allowed access to the Grotto of the Nativity.

Evidence of the turbulent history of the church can be readily seen in the fabric of the building; for centuries it was one of the most fought-over of the Holy Places. It was only by chance that this building escaped destruction during the Persian invasion of 614 A.D. It was the only major church in the country to be spared. The Persians were surprised to discover a representation of the Magi from Persia at a façade decorated with a colorful mosaic. So out of reverence and respect for their ancestors, they decided to honor these sages by sparing the church. Later, the building was seized and defended by a succession of Moslem and Crusader armies; this explains the fortress-like appearance of the church's exterior. This is also a common feature of most of the ancient religious buildings in the Holy Land. In the course of time, the complex was expanded by the addition of several chapels and monasteries belonging to different Christian Churches.

Open: Daily 5.30 a.m. to 6.30 p.m.

Description of the Church:

Today, the compound of the Nativity church covers an area of approximately 12,000 square meters and includes, besides the Basilica, the Latin convent in the north, the Greek convent in the south-east and the Armenian convent in the south-west. A bell-tower and sacristy were built adjoining the south-east corner of the Basilica. In front of the principal western entrance of the 4th century church lied the atrium of the basilica. This was a quadrangle surrounded by colonnades in the center of which were several cisterns for oblutions and baptisms. From the atrium three doors led into the vestibule of the church, but of these the central one only has been preseved.

The Door:

The main access to the Basilica is by the very small Door of Humility *(78 cm in width and 130 cm in height, 2.3 X 4.3 feet)*. Visitors must enter bending over, as if to a real cave. Originally the church had three entrances, two of which have been bricked up. They are hidden respectively by a buttress built later (after the 16th c.) and by the Armenian buildings. The central and highest portal of Justinian's church door was reshaped by the Crusaders. This resulted in a pointed arch which is still visible today; with the cornice of the Justinian entrance can be seen above. The present small entrance was made during the Ottoman era to prevent mounted horsemen

The 4th century church

from entering the Basilica. There is another small door on the northern side *(left of the main entrance)* which leads to the Franciscan convent and another small one on the southern side of the church which leads to the Greek Orthodox monastery. There are three keys which

Three Entrances

close and open the Basilica door; each community *(Catholic, Orthodox and Armenian)* has one.

The Vestibule:

Immediately past the main entrance is a vestibule, the former narthex of Justinian's imposing church. It is now bare, dark and divided into three somewhat gloomy compartments. From the vestibule a single wooden door gives access to the interior, directly into the main body of the Basilica. The panels of the door were constructed at the bidding of the Armenian king, Haytoun, in 1277, and these were made by two Armenian artists as testified by two inscriptions carved on the upper part in Arabic and Armenian.

The Interior:

The interior of the church is impressive chiefly because of its simplicity. It contains four rows of monolithic columns of Corinthian order carved from local stone. The Basilica, composed of five aisles, was kept during the Justinian rebuilding, but the western wall was moved further westward so as to lengthen the body of the church by one bay. This necessitated the demolition of Constantine's atrium and its replace-

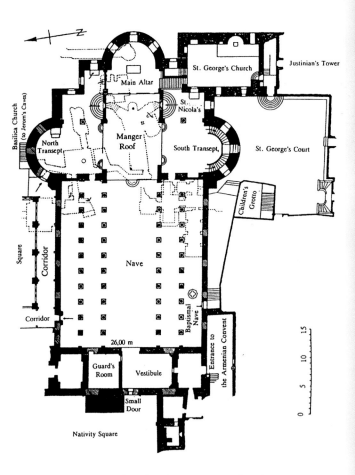

Map of the Nativity Church: the Justinian church

45

Church of the Nativity: The Nave.

ment by a new one built further west. Only a few traces now remain of the original. The Basilica is a rectangle 53.9 m. *(180 feet)* long and the nave is 26.2 m. *(94 feet)* wide and the transept 35.82 m. *(120 feet)*. The stone for the numerous golden-hued supporting columns was quarried in Bethlehem. The pillars, 44 in all, 6 meters *(20 feet)* high, and of white marble capitals are in debased Corinthian style and bear in the center of the abacus a rosette with an ornate Greek Cross. The limestone columns, which aroused the admiration of the Patriarch Sophronius, were painted during the Middle Ages with fres-

Two limestone columns painted with frescoes

coes of the Apostles; unfortunately, they have faded almost completely. A number of saints are represented on the columns with inscriptions in Greek and Latin. Among these are St. George, St. Cataldus, St. Canute, King of the Danes, and St. Olaf, King of Norway. Among the forty or so depicted some come from the Orient, others from the North. Of interest are the armorial devices sketched in the 14th and 15th centuries on the lower parts of many of the columns.

A beautiful baptismal font,

The Baptismal Font

Interior of the Church in 1918

probably of the sixth or seventh century, is seen in the south-west corner of the church; it is a monolith, octagonal in shape, with a clover-shaped tank. This location corresponds to the old baptismal rite: the catechumen arrived from the outside, received baptism and then entered the church. The unfortunate wall erected by the Greeks in 1842 at the extremity of the aisles was removed in 1918 by Sir Ronald Storrs (*British Governor*), allowing an unrestricted view of the nave, double aisles, wide transept and semi-circular apse.

The Walls:

In the central nave, there are two walls, each 9 meters high. Eleven semi-circular windows pierce the upper part of each wall, and each has a corresponding bay. The clerestory windows below the elevated roof of the nave provide a bright illumination for the church interior. There are traces of a beautiful mosaic on a gold background, dating from the second half of the twelfth century. Originally, all the inner walls of the church were covered with mosaics. The remaining mosaics on the side walls and floor attest to the former splendor of this sanctuary. The fragments of the lowest row of mosaics, still visible on the south side wall, show a series of half-figures representing the ancestors of Christ. Many others, however, are indistinguishable.

Above this row there are arcades, with altars concealed by curtains and containing the books of the Gospel. Still higher there is a Greek inscription and two Greek crosses. The in-

Fragments of the mosaics in the transept

scription is an extract from the resolution of the Council of Constantinople. This testifies that essential unity in regard to dogma existed in 1169 when the decoration of the church was brought to an end by Ephraim as it is shown by the inscription in five lines in Greek and Latin still legible in the periphery of the apse of the Choir. Above the architrave of the pillars, in spaces between the fantastic carvings of foliage, are representations of the churches of Antioch and Sardis. Others are the Resolution of the Council of Constantinople held in 381 A.D. A more remarkable remnant is still to be seen on the north side wall where the churches of Antioch and Sardica are represented. Sardica is the old name of Sophia, the capital of Bulgaria. Underneath the picture the resolution of the Council which gathered in that city in 347 A.D is written in Greek. A few others can be seen in the transepts, in the northern part: *Doubt of St. Thomas* and a part of the *Ascension of our Lord*; in the southern part, the *Triumphal Entry of Jesus* can be seen. The faded mosaics on the wall executed by the artist Ephraim, are the gift of the Emperor Manuel Camnenos, who reigned at Constantinople in the twelfth century.

The Floor:

The present floors, made of rough stone slabs, date back to the restorations made by the Greeks in 1842 who attempted to repair the damages caused by the 1834 earthquake. The mosaic floors were covered up with two feet of imported soil, and a pavement of marble slabs was laid at a higher level.

Fragments of the mosaics on the side walls

The Mosaic Floor in the Central Nave

While the church being repaired in 1934, a fine mosaic floor with a Greek inscription dating from the 4th century was discovered. This inscription read: *Ichthus* which means *fish* and also forms the initials of the five titles of Jesus: *"Jesus Christ The Son of God"*. Under some wooden boards, patches of the ancient mosaic floor can be glimpsed. In the Crusaders' time, floor marbles mirrored the brilliance of the gilded capitals.

The Roof :

Since the removal of the de-

corated flat ceiling built by Justinian, the original pointed inner roof-structure is once more visible. Since the pre-Crusader times it has been of cedar wood with the rafters exposed. The present ceiling is from the 14th century, and it was restored in 1842. The outside roof was also restored and covered with lead because in the seventeenth century the Turks decided that the lead covering the roof could be put to better use in the form of bullets.

The Transept:

Beyond the transept the five aisles reappear; the two outer ones have one bay, the inner ones have two, all ending in a straight wall. The two side arms end in a semicircular apse similar to that of the center. In front of the central apse, stands the Iconostasis which was erected by the Greeks in the 17th century. It is a decorated screen across the width of the sanctuary, separating the altar and the main body of the church. It has three doors leading to the Temple. Religious pictures and icons of Christ, the Virgin

The Iconostasis

Mary, the Apostles, Saints and others are placed on it. The present iconostasis or screen was erected in 1764 to replace an earlier screen built by Patriarch Dositheos and destroyed in 1689. It is an elaborately carved and well proportioned piece of woodwork designed in three zones each containing a series of pictures. The most interesting of these are fourteen scenes from the Gospels, painted in Byzantine style, in rectangular panels above the first cornice.

A 6-step staircase leads to the choir from where men enter the sanctuary and the presbytery. In this choir there is an artistically-carved throne used by the Greek Orthodox Patriarch or dignitaries visiting the Church. Originally the place of the present Iconostasis contained an octagonal structure covering the grotto, into which the pilgrims could probably look through a large circular opening and see the manger and the birth place without descending into the Grotto.

Justinian's architects replaced the polygonal choir area with the transept that characterizes the present edifice. They also facilitated access to the crypt by building two sets of stairs, from the two sides of the great choir, that descend to the Grotto and meet before the Altar of the Nativity.

Besides the Greeks, the Ar-

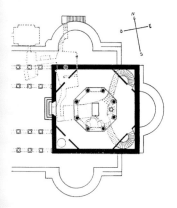

The Octagonal Structure

The Armenian Altar

thern entrance of the Cave of the Nativity, is known as the Altar of the Kings, because here, according to a popular tradition, was where the Magi or the three wise men dismounted. To the left, in the southern apse there is a small chapel of *St. Nicola*. The southern apse opens onto the courtyard of the Greek Orthodox convent used by the Anglicans for choral services on Christmas Eve. This courtyard steps lead down into a series of burial grottoes extending under the southern aisles. On the east side of the

menian Orthodox had succeeded in establishing themselves in the basilica between 1810 and 1829 and in taking possession of the northern arm of the transept. In this area there are two altars both belonging to the Armenian Church. The one in the northern apse is dedicated to the Blessed virgin; the other, beyond the nor-

Icon of the Virgin Mary in the Southern apse

Chapel of St. George

courtyard the lower part of the 12th century bell tower can be seen.

The present basilica belongs mainly to the Greek Orthodox, with shares and rights reserved for the Catholics and the Armenian Orthodox. The Protestants

The Burial Grottoes

are allowed to hold a service on Christmas Eve in the open courtyard.

The Grotto:

The part of the Church of the Nativity with the greatest religious and historical significance remains the Grotto of the Nativity, the traditional site of Jesus' birth. In the church, two entrances now lead to the Grotto. Originally, in the fourth century, there was only one entrance to the grotto from the main body of the church. An altar was erected over the birthplace, and a fourteen-pointed silver star was embedded in the

white marble to mark the traditional place of Jesus' birth. It was lit by fifteen silver lamps representing the different Christian communities. Six of the lamps belong to the Greek Orthodox, four to the Catholics, and five to the Armenian Orthodox. The star bears a Latin inscription: *Hic De Virgine Maria Jesus Christus Natus Est - 1717.* (Here Jesus Christ was

An entrance to the Grotto

The Silver Star

The Nativity Altar

born to the Virgin Mary). For Christians, the Silver Star of Bethlehem in the Grotto is a gleaming reminder of the birth of the son of God. It was installed by the Catholics in 1717, removed by the Greeks in 1847 and replaced by the Turkish government in 1853. In 1944, the medieval mosaic in the apse above the altar was cleaned and three words of the Latin text of the *Gloria in Excelsis "terra pax hominibus"* were found and they are partly preserved.

Opposite the altar of the Nativity, three steps lead the visitor to the Altar of the Manger, the place where the Baby Jesus was laid after he was born." *And she brought forth her first-born son, and wrapped him in swaddling clothes and laid him in a manger, because there was no room for them in the inn".* Here the shepherds, called by the voice of the angels and chosen by the Lord and privileged among men, knelt down, first

to adore the Child. The original clay manger according to tradition, was found by St. Helen who replaced it later with a silver manger. However, this silver manger has been preserved in the Basilica of St. Maria Maggiore in Rome since the 12th century.

A third altar has been erected opposite the Manger. It is dedicated to the Wise Men, who came from the East to Bethlehem under the guidance of a star, and *"entering into the house, found the child with Mary his mother, and falling down they adored him; and opening their treasures, they offered him gifts, gold, frankin-*

The Altar of the Manger

altar that the Catholics celebrate their services, while the Greek & Armenian Orthodox celebrate theirs at the altar of the Nativity. The remains of the three Magi were taken to Cologne in Germany in 1164. Cologne was twinned with Bethlehem in 1996.

The grotto is almost rectangular in shape measuring some 12 m. by 3 m. (*40X10 feet*) It is encased in white marble. The floor and walls are covered with slabs of marble. The grotto is

The Altar of the Magi

cense, and myrrh" (Matt. II. 1-11). It is said that this altar marks the spot where the Wise Men prostrated themselves and poured their gifts at the feet of the Infant Savior, paying homage to the new born King. The altar is adorned with paintings by Maello representing that scene. It is on this

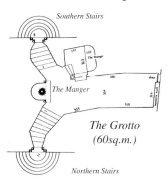

The Grotto
(60sq.m.)

Three Kings of Orient

We three kings of Orient are,
Bearing gifts we traverse afar,
Field and fountain, morr and mountain,
Following yonder Star.

O, star of wonder, star of might,
Star with royal beauty bright,
Westward leading, still proceeding,
Guide us to the perfect light.

Born a baby on Bethlehem's plan;
Gold we bring to crown Him again;
King forever, ceasing never,
Over us all to reign.

Frankincense to offer have l,
Incense owns a Deity nigh;
Prayer and praising, all men raising,
Worship Him, God on High.

Myrrh is mine, its bitter perfume,
Breathes a life of gathering gloom;
Sorrowing, sighing, bleeding, dying,
Seal'd in the stone-cold tomb.

Glorious now behold Him arise,
King and God and sacrifice,
Heaven sings, "Hallelujah!"
Hallejujah!" Earth replics.

The Adoration of the Magi by Hans Suess von Kulmbach

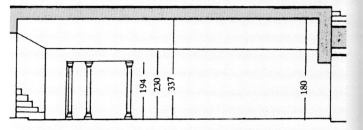

A Plan of the Grotto, Cross-section

decorated with numerous lamps, figures of saints, embroidery, and a variety of sacred ornaments. The walls of the crypt are clothed with a tapestry of amianthus which depicts the salient facts of the childhood of Jesus. The tapestry was given to the Franciscans by Macmahon, president of the French Republic. It was partly destroyed by fire in 1869. Naturally dim the crypt is lit by 53 lamps.

At the right end of the Grotto of the Nativity, we find a locked door, providing access to the grottoes adjacent to the Cave of the Nativity and associated with the early days of the church through St. Jerome and St. Paula. The Franciscans have the key to this door, but it is generally locked, except on Christmas night; the grottoes are reached by way of the

The Shrine of the Three Magi in Cologne

Franciscan church of St. Catherine. In the north-west corner of the grotto is a cistern, which has gathered about it a number of pious legends. The legend

The Cistern of the Grotto

generally associated with this cistern is that it provided water in which the Infant Jesus was washed. It was sometime confused with the well of the Magi's star which lies northeast of the place of the Nativity by the northern stairs to the cave.

St. Catherine Church:

The present Franciscan church of St. Catherine of Alexandria is entirely modern. It was built by the Franciscans in 1881 to replace the old chapel of the Augustinian Canons on the north side of the church, which was probably an adaptation of the original chapel belonging to St. Paula's convent. Little remained of this chapel when the Crusaders arrived in 1099; therefore, they built a

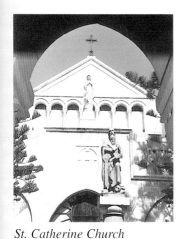

St. Catherine Church

cloister and monastery which was given to the Canons of St. Augustine and which became in 1347 a Franciscan convent.

The 12th century structure did not undergo any changes until the 18th century when this church was built. The choir was moved to the rear of the main altar and two small altars, leading to the choir, were set in chapels built for that purpose. Thus the church could house a larger audience. In 1846 a new sacristy was added. In 1880, the northern wall and the façade were removed so that the new church was wider and longer. St. Jerome's cloister lost its eastern walk. In 1949 the

St. Catherine Church, the Interior

church was further lengthened and the cloister was even further reduced in size.

The church we see today is quite modest; it is divided into three aisles by simple pillars. The interior has an aisled nave and a cross-vaulted ceiling with ribs. After entering the church from the Basilica of the Nativity, or via the cloister, you will find yourself in front of the first four pillars of the nave, previously belonging to the cloister. On your right you will see a wrought iron gate which closes the entrance to the Basilica of the Nativity. It is the work of Fr. Silverio of Cortenova and dates from the first half of the year 1700. On the right side, steps lead down to the grottos of St. Jerome.

The small arches of the *mezzanine* behind the choir and the big marble altars are more neoclassic than Romanesque. Two chapels flank the apse, dedicated respectively to St. Francis and St. Anthony. On the wall behind the Altar and above the Organ hang a remarkable picture of our Lady with the Baby

The Altar of the Immaculate Conception

Jesus surrounded by angels and St. Joseph kneeling in adoration (1800). The windows in the upper walls are decorated with geometrical motifs; the ones along the aisles and over the door are of stained glass.

St. Catherine's Church is familiar to many people because it is the one used for Midnight Christmas Mass. Under the altar of the Immaculate Conception (southern wall) you will see the statue of the Infant carried during the Christmas procession . Every Christmas,

Our Lady with Baby Jesus in St. Catherine Church

upon completion of the Midnight Mass, the Patriarch of Jerusalem, leading a procession, takes this infant down to the Nativity grotto and lays it first on the silver star, then in the Manger. The daily procession of Franciscan Fathers from the church to the Basilica at noon, is well worth watching. It is one of the few times when an air of solemnity seems to take hold of Bethlehem.

Among the artistic items of bygone times is the baptismal font (*1734*). A fine panel wooden door admits one to the convent (northern side). The new front door is decorated with four bas-relief bronze panels representing St. Jerome, St. Eusebius, Paula and Eustochium. They are the work of Prof. A. Mortet. A marble statue of Our Lady dominates the cloister from the top of the church façade. The bell tower does not belong to a well defined style. The five big bells were cast at Bassano, Italy in 1882 and 1887. The church was designed by Architect Cuillemot. The fame of this church rests on the solemn Roman Catholic midnight mass celebrated there on Christmas Eve. The midnight mass is broadcast live, by satellite to TV networks all over the world. The church is under construction now. In an attempt to enlarge the church, the altars of St. Francis and St. Anthony were knocked down and will be moved 15 meters to the back. The work is expected to be finished by Christmas 1998. Another Church under St. Catherine's from the Crusaders period was restored in 1997 in order to create more space for the celebrations of the year 2000.

Cloister of St. Jerome:

The cloister was accidentally revealed by a fire, which destroyed some modern rubble and plaster work that had masked the archway of the 12th century structure. It was restored in 1947 by Architect A. Burluzzi. Now, this cloister is the most outstanding example of a Medieval cloister. There are four bays in each walk of the cloister and each bay originally opened to the central area through a triple arcaded entrance. Only some arches and a fragment of a three-mullioned bay are still standing. The remainder has disappeared. The 1947 restoration plans had to

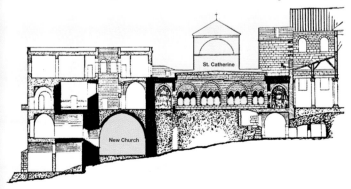

Cross-section: St. Catherine Church and the underground church

Cloister of St. Jerome

take into account the incorporation of a section of this cloister into the church. Thus, the cloister suffered a second reduction after the one made in 1880 to enlarge the church.

The old design was respected in order to maintain the austere character of the 12th century work. The carving of the capitals, which combines acanthus motives with animal forms, is a characteristic of French 12th century work. The ancient cloister had 64 geminated capitals of *nary stone* (soft grain). Only 20 of them survived and are more or less well preserved. All 20 were reused and the destroyed ones were replaced with new uncarved capitals merely reproducing the outline. In spite of their lamentable condition, the surviving capitals betray a remarkable artistic quality, expressive of that historical period. Now, we can see a cloister of perfect proportions and nobody would guess that it is a reconstruction.

In the center of the cloister, stands a pillar crowned by a capital of white stone with the sculptured figure of St. Jerome. It dates from 1880, but in the 1947 restoration a most unbe-

Cloister of St. Jerome

St. Jerome's cell

coming lime covering had to be removed. The skull under the Saint's foot symbolizes the severity of the ascetic life. St. Jerome came in 384 A.D. with a group of pilgrims to settle in Bethlehem. Two years later, two Roman ladies of noble birth St. Paula and her daughter, St. Eustochium, arrived and founded a western monastic tradition in Bethlehem which has endured with interruptions, till this day. St. Paula built two monasteries, one for St. Jerome and his friends and the other for herself and her companions who came from Rome. She also built a big hospice for pilgrims.

Here, St. Jerome (*Hyronimus*) spent the rest of his life and produced his great literary works, among them his Latin Translation of the Old Testament now known as the Vulgate. Thus, St. Jerome became the Patron of translators all over the world. The International Federation of Translators celebrates on September 30, the International Day of Translation; St. Jerome's feast day. He died in 420 and his remains were transferred first by Theodosius II to Constantinople, and later to Santa Maria Maggiore in Rome.

In the cloister's southern walk, under a gate we see the Medieval staircase leading to St. Jerome's oratory and the old entrance admitting one to the basilica. The later was reduced in size due to reasons of safety. The discovery of traces of an entrance with a threshold confirms an earlier theory that these caves formed the original entrance to the Grotto of the Nativity and constituted the outer part of it.

Adjacent Grottoes to the Cave of the Nativity:

There is a network of caves through which the Church of St. Catherine can be reached from the Grotto of the Nativity. A visitor goes down to the Grottoes through a small staircase to the right of the entrance in St. Catherine's, which opens under the Basilica's northern apse. The first cave is dedicated to the *Holy Innocents*, who because of the fury of Herod were the first to shed their blood for Christ. In the Middle Ages this was believed to be the refuge of the mothers of the Innocents, and in later years as the place where the massacred bodies were thrown. The main altar in this impressive subterranean complex is devoted to *St. Joseph* in memory of his vision. It is south of the cave of the Holy Innocents, and at a higher level. It was here that St. Joseph is said to have had the dream which caused his fateful decision to flee to Egypt, in order to safeguard the child that had been entrusted in his care. Beyond this crooked cut rock, a passage leads up to the door at the western extremity of the cave of the Nativity, where you can look through the keyhole, and see the Nativity altar. Near the end of this passage, on the right hand side, the blocked up western entrance to the crypts can be seen.

Returning now to the Chapel of the Innocents, you can see a passage on the left which leads to the tomb of St. Jerome. On the right hand side of the passage is an altar dedicated to Eusebius of Cremona, a pupil of St. Jerome and his successor as superior of the monastery. The chamber, which the above passage leads to, contains two altars. The further one is above the traditional tomb of *St. Jerome*. The altar on the opposite side of the chapel covers the tomb of *Sts. Paula and Eustochium*. In front of the tomb there is an ancient cistern. The innermost grotto is St. Jerome's cell, where he isolated himself during his literary activity. Here he spent his time translating and commenting on the Bible. He also translated into Latin the *Onomasticon* a record of place-names in Palestine, which had been written in Greek by Eusebius, the bishop of Caesarea, in about 360 A.D. This chapel is lit by the ancient staircase leading to the southern walk of the cloister.

The Armenian Monastery:

To the south of the forecourt of the Church of the Nativity

The Armenian Convent

The Armenian Church Steeple

lies the Armenian Monastery. The building is of various periods and incorporates a substantial nucleus of constructions dating from the Byzantine and Crusader periods. Within the monastery one can also find traces of Justinian's atrium. The monastery in its present shape antedates the Crusader's epoch, which allows the visitor to visualize the dimensions of the original Church of the Nativity.

If you walk out of the church into the narthex by the main western door and turn to the left, you can go through a door that leads into the southern end of the narthex. You can see on the right a second door leading into a private room belonging to the monastery. This room is built in the south-east corner of Justinian's cloister. At the south end of the narthex there is a door leading out into a small open courtyard containing a cistern; the water of this well is believed by pilgrims to have curative properties. On the right-hand side is a flight of stairs, providing access to the inhabi-ted part of the monastery. It is usually possible to find one of the monks or servants of the monastery to show you such parts of the building that are of interest.

The Armenian monastery was once a major center for Armenian hermits. The most important period of monasticism was during the pontificate of the great ascetic Patriarch Krikor Baronder in the 17th century when scribes here were active in the copying and illustrating Bibles. The monastery now houses only six monks and provides community services for Bethlehem's six hundred Armenians. The Monastery church of *St. Jacob* is decorated with blue tiles, and the three altars are sculptured in wood; there is also an eighteenth-century painting depicting the Baptism of Christ. It is also famous for an old baptismal font where many pilgrims vowed to have their children baptized. Patriarch Krikor Baronder converted the great refectory, which was previously a stable, into a church in the name of the Holy Trinity. He built two altars to the right and left, and dedicated them to the sons of Zebedee. Yet a short time later the church was again converted into a refectory.

Overlooking Manger Square, the roof of the monastery offers a unique panoramic view of Bethlehem with its terraced environs. The Armenian church steeple, built in 1935, overlooks Manger square.

School of St. Jerome:

One of the interesting places in the Armenian monastery is

the school of St. Jerome. This twelfth-century structure consists of a long hall with two parallel rows of cross-vaults supported by a row of five columns down the middle with Byzantinian capitals. It is believed that St. Jerome taught his disciples under the high vaults of the colonnaded hall. It has now been divided into two stories by a floor inserted at the springing of the vaults. The upper part of the two stories is used as a refectory, and the lower is in disuse. Some of the capitals of the columns appear protruding from the floor of the refectory; they were probably taken by the Crusaders from the ruins of Justinian's atrium.

In the basement you may observe the stable which housed the horses of the exhausted pilgrims who stayed overnight. In the corner, there is an obsolute olive-press with huge stones. There are underground water cisterns of great antiquity and one particular well is reputed by local tradition to have curative qualities.

Within the complex of the Armenian monastery you can study the ancient methods of

The Greek Othodox Convent

stone-dressing and trace a continuity of stone-laying traditions. For example, an early Byzantine wall alongside Justinian structures, and the foundations of a Crusader tower, are topped with an early Ottoman superstructure.

Greek Orthodox Convent:

The part of the Church of the Nativity which is under the control of the Greek Orthodox is supervised and defended by a Bishop or an Archimandrite as well as assistants including deacons and monks. All of them are Greeks and live in the Greek Orthodox Convent adjacent to the Church from the

The Greek Othodox Convent

south-east. The building is of various periods and incorporates a substantial nucleus of constructions. In the middle of the south apse of the Church of Nativity, is a door which gives access to a courtyard of the Greek Convent. The east side of the yard is closed by the massive wall of the sacristy and of the old bell tower. The lower part of the walls dates back to Justinian's time or before; some of this masonry may represent the base of the tower that protected the monasteries in early Byzantine times. The upper part was rebuilt in Crusader times as a bell tower. The top of the tower now includes mixed medieval and nineteenth century work. At the foot of the tower, adjoining the church, is the old Sacristy, a twelfth-century structure, now the Chapel of St. George. It can be reached directly from the church by a flight of steps leading up from the Sanctuary. At the opposite side of the court a flight of stairs behind an iron gate leads down into a series of burial grottoes extending under the southern aisles and nave of the church. The upper part of the present building on the south of the yard dates back to 1948. Part of the upper floor of the Greek Orthodox Convent serves as a residence for President Arafat when he visits Bethlehem since its liberation on December 22, 1995.

The Casa Nova:

The Casa Nova is the Franciscan pilgrims' hostel. In the year 1908, the "Old House" as it had come to be known, was replaced by a new structure which afforded hospitality to Pilgrims and housed the Parish Boys' School. It was built in place of the Augustinian convent on the slopes of the hill and is composed of a many storied building. From 1347 until now, the Franciscan Fathers have brought about some necessary changes, but the general lines of the monastery are well preserved. In 1980 the same building was renovated. A new parish school *Terra Sancta College* was built in 1965 in front of the Casa Nova.

The Casa Nova

Sites Around the Town

Mosaic Map of Bethlehem in the Cloister of St. Jerome

Milk Grotto:

A few minutes walk from the Church of the Nativity, to the southeast of the basilica, brings you to a cave known as the Milk Grotto. You can reach it by following the narrow Milk Grotto Street which starts at the corner of Manger Square, or through the door in the Basilica's southern apse which takes

The Holy Family: Carved Stone by Local Artists

you almost to the mid-way point of the Milk Grotto street. The grotto is of irregular shape hollowed out of the soft white rock. It is now converted into a chapel called by the local Christians "*Magharet Sitti Mariam* (The Grotto of the Lady Mary), but more commonly known to Westerners as the Milk Grotto. A church was built here, probably by St. Paula, at least before the fifth century. There are mosaic fragments on the terrace of the grotto, likely belonging to the 5th century, with geometrical motifs and crosses on them. This Grotto was transformed later into a lavishly decorated Chapel.

Tradition has it that the Blessed Virgin stayed for a short time in this Grotto with the divine child. St. Joseph, informed by an angel of the danger threatening the Child and of the need to flee to Egypt, began at once to get ready for the journey and hurried up Mary, who was nursing the Child. A few drops of milk fell on the ground and suddenly the red rock turned white.

This ancient sanctuary is very much venerated by Christians of all rites and even by Muslims. For many centuries, Christian and Muslim women have entertained a belief that the rock had acquired curative properties. If while nursing mothers lack milk, they go to the grotto and, having prayed there, they take a piece of the soft rock, which they grind into powder and mix with their drink. It was customary for European pilgrims to chip off tiny pieces from the whitish rock and take

Rest on the flight to Egypt by Joachim Patenier

them to the churches in their own towns. From this Grotto came those soft white stones to

Entrance of the Milk Grotto

be found in many European churches under the name of The Virgin's Milk. The earliest record of this practice is in the 7th century.

The present building around the grotto was erected by the Franciscans in 1872. Some mosaics, and traces of walls from the old church still remain. The façade of the church is a fine example of native workman-

Mary nursing Baby Jesus

ship: the Nativity and the Flight to Egypt are told in stone by local artists on the capitals of columns. The stone was carved as if it were mother-of-pearl. The small façade, donated by local Christians, is a nice example of native craftsmanship (1935).

Local artisans have shown their love and devotion for the site by building a staircase with a mother-of-pearl inlay. Inside the Grotto, in a cozy corner we find unique paintings of the Virgin nursing the Child. The people of Bethlehem have additionally expressed their devotion by decorating the chapel with mother-of-pearl carvings. Also remarkable is the small arch midway up the staircase, rendered fine by alternate white and red stones. To go up to the terrace you have to ring the bell. A Franciscan Father will let you in. He keeps also the key of St. Joseph's Chapel.
Open: Daily 8.00-11.45 a.m., 2.00-6.00 p.m. Tel: 743867

The House of St. Joseph:
(St. Joseph Chapel)

Continuing down the road, after a few minutes we find the House of St. Joseph on the right. In the present chapel, built by the Franciscans in 1892, we can see remains of the primitive church in the lower layer of the apse embedded in the rock and the base of the ancient altar.

The Holy Family lived here until the flight into Egypt. It is here the Magi found the Child with Mary his Mother *(Matt. 2,11)*.

King David's Well:

On Star Street, a few minutes walk from Manger Square and inside the premises of the *Catholic Action Club,* there are three large cisterns, still in use, hewn in the rock; they are the cisterns of David mentioned in the Bible *(2 Sm 23, 15-17).* The wells mark the site where David's followers broke through the Philistine lines in order to fetch him drinking water from the well of Bethlehem. David and his 400 men were in the *Cave of Adullam,* when Bethlehem was garrisoned by the

King David's Well

Philistines. He expressed the desire to drink water of the Well of Bethlehem, which is by the gate. The wish was overheard by three of David's bodyguards who set out to grant the desire of their master. Breaking through the Philistine lines, they secured the precious water and returned with it to the cave. But David refused to drink the water for which the lives of his followers had been endangered, and "poured it out unto the Lord". *(2 Samuel 23, 14-16)*. The three large cisterns are the only monument in Bethlehem to the famous king who was born here. Beyond the cisterns there are also remnants of a church founded by St. Paula and an underground cemetery. In 1895 a fragment of a fine mosaic pavement belonging to the church was found. In the Byzantine era, between the fourth and sixth century, a convent and church were built on the site. The church was decorated with mosaics which incorporated a quotation from Psalm 118: "*Open to me the gates of righteousness; I will go into them and I will praise the Lord. This is the gate of the Lord, into which the righteous shall enter*". It was customary to carve these verses on doors of churches. The monks serving in the church were buried in catacombs under the building, and the names of some of them can still be seen on the tombs, e.g. Constantine the Deacon, Cyrus, Theodore and Eugene. There are eighty of these tombs. An oil lamp made of clay was placed near each grave and was lit each year on the feast day of the monk.

Open: 8.00-12.00 a.m.,
*   12.30-20.00 p.m.*
Monday through Saturday
Tel: 743277, 742477

Rachel's Tomb:

Near the entrance to Bethlehem, you see the dome of Rachel, the sepulcher of Jacob's beloved spouse who died giving birth to their son Benjamin. The Bible relates: "*And they journeyed from Beth El; and there was still some way to come to Ephrath. And Rachel died, and was buried in the way to Eph-*

Rachel's Tomb

rath. *And Jacob set up a pillar upon her grave: the same is the pillar of Rachel's grave unto this day" (Gen 16-20).* The tomb of Rachel has been renowned throughout the ages. The Crusaders built a square structure over the gray tomb, with twelve arches and a cupola. The simple building which houses the tomb today was erected by the Turks in 1620, since then the monument has been repeatedly restored. In 1788, the arches were filled. In 1841, Sir Moses Montefiore secured the key of the tomb for the use of the Jews, added a square vestibule with a *Mihrab* or praying-place for Muslims, and rebuilt a dome over the tomb. For many centuries the tomb was marked by a pyramid of twelve stones;

A Muslim cemetery near the tomb of Rachel (1850)

each stone represents one of the tribes of Israel. The tomb was probably a natural cave.

Rachel's tomb is one of the few shrines which Muslims, Jews and Christians agree in honoring, and about which their traditions are identical. Superstitious Jewish women hang threads round the tomb of *"Our Mother Rachel"* and wind them around the wrists of their daughters, to bring them healthy sons. From 1948 to 1967 the site was under the protection of the Islamic *Waqf* and was open to Jewish worshippers. Today it is under permanent guard by Israeli soldiers. The tomb is now in the possession of the Israelis and a modern building is under construction around it; it is visited by many pilgrims.

In addition, the image of Rachel weeping represents the sorrow of the mothers of Bethlehem who had lost their babies: *"Then was fulfilled that which was spoken by Jeremiah the prophet, saying; A voice in Rama was heard, lamentation and great mourning; Rachel bewail-*

ing her children, and would not be comforted, because they are not"(Matt. II 17). Rachel is represented as rising from her tomb and weeping for her children who had to suffer death on account of the new-born King.

Open: Sun-Thus 8.00-Sunset
Fri: 8.00 a.m. -1.00 p.m.
It can be reached by bus or car from Jerusalem or the Manger Square.

The Aqueducts:

On the outskirts of Bethlehem, there remains traces of two Roman aqueducts. The older one was built under Pontius Pilatus, procurator of Judea *(26-36 A.D)*. It started near *'Ain 'Arrub*, ran along the hillsides past Solomon's pools, reached Bethlehem through a tunnel, and then Jerusalem up to the *al-Haram* area. This aqueduct, restored and repaired, continued to bring water to Jerusalem until 1947. The construction of this aqueduct gave Bethlehem a permanent supply of running water for the first time. In the middle ages it was known as the *River of Tekoah* because it passed through the land of that village. It was probably repaired by the Ayyubid Sultan *al-Malek al-'Adil*, to bring water to al-Haram ash-Sharif in the 12th century A.D. Remnants of this aqueduct lie in an abandoned cave some 400 m. from the crossroad to Hebron, near Rachel's Tomb.

The second aqueduct was built at the end of the second century under Emperor Septimius Severus by the soldiers of the 10th Legion, *the Fretensis*. Water was conveyed from a source called *Bir ed-Daragi*, not far from Solomon's pools; some sections run on level ground. The aqueduct was formed by cubic blocks of white limestone. Its remnants, also not far from Rachel's tomb, are found in the triangle formed by the fork of the road leading to Manger Street.

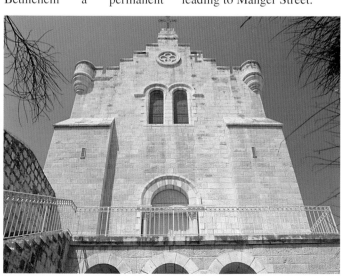

The Chapel of the Carmelites

Around Bethlehem

Shepherds on the Outskirts of Bethlehem

THE SHEPHERDS' FIELD

According to an ancient tradition, the Shepherds received the first tidings of the Nativity in a broad valley in Beit Sahour: *And there were in the same country shepherds abiding in the field, keeping watch over their flock by night. And the angel said unto them, "Fear not: for, behold, I bring you good tidings of great joy, which shall be to all people. For unto you is born this day in the city of David a Savior, which is Christ the Lord. And this shall be a sign unto you: Ye shall find the baby wrapped in swaddling clothes, lying in a manger". And suddenly there was with the angel a multitude of the heavenly host praising God, and saying, "Glory to God in the highest, and on earth peace, good will toward men". And it came to pass, as the angels were gone away from them into heaven, the shepherds said one to another, "Let us now go even unto Bethlehem, and see this thing which is come to pass, which the Lord hath made known unto us." (Luke 2:8-15).*

The Shepherds by Le Nain

The precise location of the appearance of the angels to the shepherds is unknown, but several sites have been venerated by Christians at different periods. St. Jerome *(347-420 A.D.)* believed the field to be identical with that in which Jacob, long before, had spread his tent, beyond the tower of Eder *(Genesis 35, 21)*. He also tells us that the tower itself lay about a thousand paces to the east of Bethlehem. Not long after St. Jerome's time, a church was built nearby. Arculfus *(670 A.D.)* a french bishop, who traveled to the Holy Land and toured it for about nine months, related to his host of Iona that he himself visited this church which contained the tombs of the three shepherds. For centuries, a monastery stood on the spot, but there is no mention of a cave until the Crusaders' time *(1099-1187)*. The tradition of the site, which goes back to the time of the Roman Paula, centered on two: one is in the care of the Greek Orthodox Church known as *Der Er-Ra'wat*, and the other is maintained by the Franciscans and known as *Der Es-Siar.*

The Orthodox Shepherds' Field:

This site is located in a small valley with olive trees, some dating back 2000 years. It is a subterranean church dedicated to the Mother of God. Local Christians call the site *Der Er-Ra'wat* meaning Convent of the Shepherds. In Greek the site is known simply as *Poemenion* meaning the *pasture*. The site is revered as the spot where an angel surrounded by a supernatural light, appeared to the bewildered shepherds and sang: *"Glory to God in the highest: and on earth peace to men of good will"*. Three of the shepherds to whom the angel announced the birth of Christ were buried in the west side of the Cave Church; their tomb is still visible today. The Shepherds had as a provision of

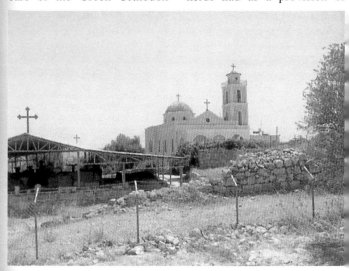

The Orthodox Shepherds' Field

The Shepherd's tomb

their last will and testament that they be buried in the place where they heard the angelic proclamation.

Over this cave, St. Helena built a church and beside it a convent for nuns, called the Convent of the *Gloria in Excelsis.* Today, only the crypt of the church remains. One descends a flight of twenty-four

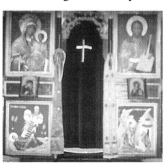

Old paintings in the underground crypt

steps into it. It is a dark, subterranean chapel which contains an altar at the east with a number of paintings and a small apse behind it. The roof is a cut stone vault of the usual Roman or Byzantine type. Some fragments of a mosaic pavement can be seen on the floor and faint traces of painting on the walls. However, the painting is not easy to view in the gloomy light of the chapel. An opening high up in the west end of the north wall leads into a second vaulted crypt of an unknown purpose. It was probably used at one time as a cistern, but has since been converted into a chapel commemorating the appearance of the angles to the shepherds. The few ruins in the vicinity probably belong to the Church of the *Gloria in Excelsis.* The crypt of the church is still in use, and the key is kept by the Greek priest in Beit Sahour whose help is required to visit the church.

The New Church:

A new Church, was erected near the traditional site of the underground Church of the Shepherds. *Archimandrite Sera-*

Iconostasis of the new church

phim, spiritual father of the Monastery of Mar Sabas, built in 1972 a modern, full-sized church above the Cave Church. Excavating the foundations for the new, he found remains of three different churches of the fifth, sixth and seventh centuries. To preserve these precious remains, it was decided to build the new church adjacent to rather than immediately above the cave. The new church has three holy altars which are dedicated as follows: the main altar to the Mother of God, the altar on the right to the great martyr and healer, Saint Panteleimon, and the altar on the left side to the archangels Michael and Gabriel and all the heavenly hosts.

Open: 8.00–11.00 a.m.,
13.00–17.00 p.m.,
Tel: 6473135

The Catholic Shepherds' Field:

Another site revered by tradition is known as *Der Es-Siar* (Sheepfold). This site lies 1 km (*0.6 mile*) to the north-west of the Church of *Er-Ra'wat*. It belongs to the Franciscan

A church inside a cave in Der Es-Siar

Fathers and was carefully excavated, revealing a vast monastic agricultural establishment, cisterns and grottoes. According to evidence in the field, an early church dating from the 5th century was enlarged in the 6th century, and stones from the octagonal construction of the Basilica of the Nativity were employed in the construction of its apse. The most striking of the remains at *Es-Siar* is a fine arched cistern in perfect condition. There are also Byzantine remains of mosaic floors, water channels, wine-vats, and

A cave with an altar in Der Es-Siar

the ruins of a group of buildings that suggest a farmstead rather than a specifically monastic establishment.

Among the rooms of the second monastery a few were identified as used for particular purposes: a porter's lodge, a bakery with a big basalt millstone, a refectory, an oil press, a cave-cellar and a stable. Also a canalization system and several cisterns were brought to light. Nearby, there are the remains of a watch-tower, known as Eder Tower (Tower of the Flocks), which is now incorporated in the Franciscan Hospice.

The Tower of the Flocks

The cave with an altar was traditionally considered as having been inhabited by the Shepherds. It is possible that these ruins are from the monastery in which Posidonius lodged in the year 400, beyond the Shepherds' monastery. Eusebius of Caesarea, bishop and scholar, writes that the Eder Tower, a thousand paces from Bethlehem, marked the place where the shepherds received the message. This was understood to be the Migdal Eder mentioned in the Old Testament *(Genesis 35:21)*. Just below the valley to the north of the Franciscan convent, is a Greek Orthodox building known as *Little Mar Sabas*, where a monk lives to care for the surrounding olive groves.

The New Church:

The present sanctuary, which was erected in 1953-54, stands over a cave in which the shepherds are supposed to have lived. It is built in the shape of a tent, a polygon with five straight and five projecting sides. The light which floods the interior reminds one of the strong light present when the angels announced the divine birth. Inside the church, the frontal and the upper part of the altar are decorated with fifteen panels depicting various scenes from the Annunciation to the arrival of the Holy Family in Egypt. The bronze high-relief on the door lintel was designed by sculptor D. Cambellotti who also created the portal, candlesticks, crosses

The Shepherds' Field: The new church

Christmas Carols to celebrate the joyous event.

Open: 8.00–11.00 a.m.,
14.00–17.00 p.m.,
Tel: 02 6472413

BEIT SAHOUR

There are two towns in close proximity to Bethlehem: Beit Sahour and Beit Jala, each with a population of 14,000 inhabitants. Today, they seem like extensions of Bethlehem; no municipal boundaries divide them. The Shepherds' Field is located in Beit Sahour (*the house of vigilance*). Its name reportedly stems from the Canaanite words "*beet*" meaning place, and "*Sahour*" meaning night watch. The name reflects the town's importance for shepherds as a grazing site during daytime and the safety of the abundant caves offered to the flocks at night. It has a pastoral setting and the olive groves dominate the horizon. This town can be reached on foot from Bethlehem by way of the Milk Grotto street. Visitors can observe here the general slope of the land

Altar of the Shepherds

and the four bronze statues supporting the main altar in the middle of the chapel. Arch. U. Noni frescoed the three apses, and sculptor A. Minghette cared for the execution of the ten stucco angels on the dome. The Church was designed by the celebrated architect, Barluzzi, and both the laying of the foundation stone and the dedication took place on a Christmas Day. Every year at Christmas Eve and Christmas Day, these fields are crowded with thousands of pilgrims, singing

Beit Sahour with the Shepherds' Fields: 1. Es-Siar 2. Er-Ra'wat

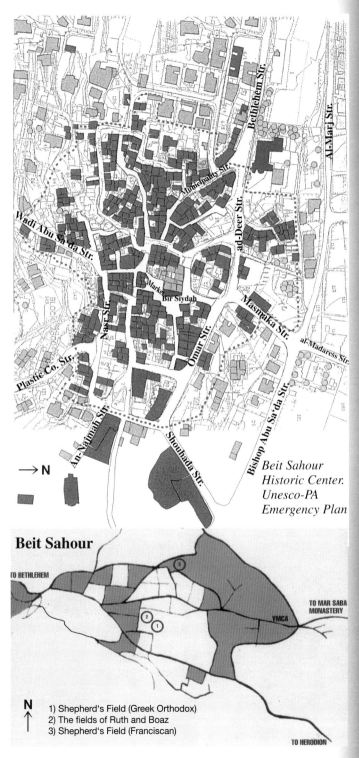

Beit Sahour Historic Center. Unesco-PA Emergency Plan

Beit Sahour

1) Shepherd's Field (Greek Orthodox)
2) The fields of Ruth and Boaz
3) Shepherd's Field (Franciscan)

eastward, on the farthest decline of which lies the town, and how they finally terminate in a small plain in the midst of which lies the shepherds' field.

Beit Sahour has origins going back to the Bronze Age (*3000 B.C.*) The Canaanites inhabited its numerous caves. Traces of inhabitants were found in caves, going back to Roman times. The remnants of very ancient oil presses found under the foundations of the two monasteries, demonstrate beyond every doubt that the place was inhabited at the time when Jesus was born in Bethlehem. Oral traditions still in circulation assert that many Christian families who came from Yemen and *Wadi Musa* in Jordan in the middle of the 14th century took shelter in Beit Sahour. In the sixteenth century, houses rose up the mountain slope between the shepherds' field and the Nativity hill. Then, it spread to the site of the present Municipal Market near *"Bir-Essyydah"* the Well of Mary.

Today, Beit Sahour is a Christian town with a Muslim minority. It is a middle class place and a thriving town with many industries: plastics, olive wood, clothing and mother-of-pearl. It has gained a reputation as a high-tech manufacturing center, the West Bank's "silicon valley". However, owing to the cruel events that befell the town after the civil disobedience reflecting the residents' refusal of and resistance to the Israeli

Beit Sahour Town Center

occupation, many businesses and small factories were confiscated. The town center has narrow thoroughfares, with houses built of polished *sandstone*, parts of which date back to the sixteenth and seventeenth cen-

Beit Sahour in the 17th century

The Latin Church, the Mosque and the Orthodox Church

turies. Some of its roads are topped by rocky arches supported by the house walls, reflecting the charm of the architecture in those days. The buildings are rarely more than two or three stories high. Modern Beit Sahour has many beautiful villas and buildings with many stories.

Beit Sahour is the home of many fine churches. The Latin Patriarchate has a church with a very ornate altar, built in 1859. The church was erected by Father Jean Muretan. In 1951, it was completely transformed by Arch. A. Barluzzi and was consecrated and dedicated to our *Lady of Fatima* and *St. Theresa of Lisieux*. The fine portico of the church has three pointed arches; the upper part of the façade is crowned by a flight of slender little arches which also run along the side walls. The inside is divided into a nave and two aisles by two rows of four columns each. The very narrow pointed arches create the illusion that the inside is longer than it actually is. The main altar is

The Altar of the Latin Church

especially worth mentioning. In spite of its size, it looks like an ivory miniature rather than carved stone. The frontal and the upper part of the altar are decorated with 15 panels representing various scenes from the Annunciation to the arrival of the Holy Family in Egypt. At the same level at the tabernacle, there are four little statues of the Evangelists; in the upper part, the 12 Apostles surround the image of Christ. Builders of this work were Palestinian artists from the town. Near the church there is a school run by the Rosary Sisters, as well as a large hall for the parish activities, and a club for the parish scouts.

Within the town, there is a Greek Orthodox church built in 1897. The Greek Orthodox represent the majority of the population. Before this church was built, the underground church in the Shepherds' field was used. Another church was built in 1972 near the site of the Shepherds' Field, and a new

A Panel from the Altar

secondary school was built in 1990 adjacent to the church. The Arab Orthodox Club is the oldest club in the town; it was founded in 1924 and its scout group is the largest in town.

The Greek Catholic community represents 15% of the population. They have a church, a school and a small seminary run by the Salvatorian Fathers of Lebanon and the Salvatorian

Greek Catholic Convent and School

82

Sisters who arrived in 1958 to look after the seminary. The Lutherans have a church and a secondary school established since 1901. Adjacent to the school is the Center of Alternative Tourism. The Muslims have a mosque, built in 1954, and the Islamic Society runs a nursery, a cultural center and two clubs. In Beit Sahour there are three boy scout groups and different clubs for youth. One club is a Cultural Center for the Children, initiated in 1992 by a group of women to develop the child's cultural and intellectual abilities. The Center is on Doha Street in front of the playground of the Public Secondary School for Boys which is used as an airport for President Arafat's helicopters when he visits Bethlehem.

Among the most important institutions and centers in Beit Sahour are: The Fashion and Textile Institute, founded in 1994 as a leading institute in the field of training middle cadres for the garment industry. Training is offered in fashion design and pattern making. There is also a Palestinian Center for Public Opinion, founded in 1994, dedicated to conducting public opinion surveys. The center holds seminars and workshops on topics of interest to the public to enhance their awareness of human rights.

There is also a Center for Rapprochement Between Peoples. It brings Palestinians and people from different nationalities, on a grass-roots level. Together they discuss and try to overcome stereotypes, prejudice and fears in order to bring about a better understanding and readiness to advocate a just and peaceful solution of the Palestinian cause. The emphasis of the Center's work is on facilitating dialogue between Palestinians and Israelis. It started its activities in 1988, under the auspices of the Mennonite Central Committee in Jerusalem.

The Alternative Tourism Group is another center which offers groups or individuals a unique opportunity to experience the Holy Land and the

The Rehabilitation Center

local Palestinian culture, away from the tourist crowds and waiting lines. It provides streamlined itineraries created to meet the specific needs and preferences of the visiting group.

A rehabilitation center for the victims of the *Intifada* (Palestinian uprising against the Israeli occupation) was established in 1989. The program focuses on counseling dimensions in rehabilitation to help the physically handicapped to cope with their new conditions, to adjust to their social environment, and to promote awareness among the people toward the needs and rights of the handicapped. The center consists of a counseling unit, and a vocational training unit including carpentry, upholstery, tailoring, computers, secretarial work and art.

The inhabitants of Beit Sahour were widely known during the Intifada in 1988, for their tax resistance movement against the Israeli occupation. When the tax disobedience started, the inhabitants raised the slogan *No Taxation Without Representation;* the same slogan the Boston Tea Party raised. The occupation authorities began an all-out campaign to crush the tax resistance with widespread raids, arrests, curfews and confiscation of commercial and private properties of the people of Beit Sahour. The curfew lasted forty-five days. In the last days a resolution was introduced in the United Nations Security Council calling upon Israel to stop the tax raids and to return all the confiscated goods, which were never returned.

Field of Ruth:

The Shepherds' Field is also the site of the meeting of Boaz and Ruth recounted in the Book of Ruth. Somewhere in this area the lyrical tale of Naomi and Ruth, gleaning in the barley fields of Bethlehem

The Field of Ruth

took place. Moreover, it has left an indelible mark on the minds of countless generations. Ruth is unique in the history of womankind because her story is not primarily that of her love for a man, but of her devotion to her mother-in-law. Ruth was married to Boaz and had a son *Obed* whose son, Jesse, was the father of David, the King and Prophet.

Bir as-Sydah :
(The Well of the Lady)

There are several grottoes and cisterns in Beit Sahour. Bir as-Sydah, situated in the center of town, is the deepest and most important. Jacob, the son of Isaac who was Abraham's son, was the one who dug it.

Bir as-Sydah Chapel

The Virgin Mary, while on her way to Egypt, passed by it and being thirsty, she asked to be given a drink from a pail of water, because the well was deep. The inhabitants refused to draw water for the Virgin, and the water rose in the well on its own accord. This cistern is famous as the scene of traditional miracles. It had been the site of the visitation by Virgin Mary. It is a religious endowment be-

longing to the whole town. The Municipality has built a shrine over the cistern expressly for the use of Christians of all denominations. It is also revered by many Muslims. Inside, the walls are covered with icons and paintings of Christian subjects given by worshippers; but profusely and randomly scattered among these, are a significant number of gifts and pictures.

Visiting hours: 8-12 a.m.
Monday through Saturday.

BEIT JALA

Beit Jala, 2 kms (*1.24 mile*) from Bethlehem, is an old Canaanite city whose name in Aramaic means "grass carpet". It is also known as Galem in the Greek version of Joshua (*XV.60*). However, it is believed by some authorities to be *"Giloh"*, the native place of "Ahitophel", the counselor of King David. The town lies on the slope of a hill covered with olive trees and vineyards and is famous for the tasty apricots grown there. The town is reputed for its master stone-masons. Its sculptors have left their mark on many buildings and tombstones in Jerusalem and Bethlehem.

There are many places of interest worth visiting in this Christian town. Beit Jala is the home of many churches, the most famous being the church of *Mar Nichola* (St. Nicholas) with its square tower and glittering dome, and the Church of the Virgin. Both belong to the Greek Orthodox denomination and are situated in the town center. The present *Mar Nicola* church was founded on the site of the old cave inhabited by St.

Beit Jala: Panoramic view of the Ras Mountain

Nicholas who came from Cappadocia in Asia Minor.

The Latin Patriarchate occupies a cluster near *al-Manshia* Square which includes the Parish Church, a secondary school run by the Rosary Sisters, a seminary and the Theological Studies Institute, a branch of the *Lateran University* in Rome. The Patriarchal seminary was founded in 1848. The present monastery was built in 1930. Enlarged considerably during the past 20 years, it now has a Junior and Senior Seminary. From 1848 till 1997 the Seminary prepared 250 priests, 85 of them work today in the local parishes. The preparation of candidates to priesthood in the Senior Seminary needs seven years of studies in philosophy and theology.

On the hill higher up on the Virgin St., there is a Lutheran church and a school, a mosque and the Arab Orthodox Club. Passing through town along *ash-Sharafa* Street to the top of the hill, there is a road on the right which leads to Cremisan where the Salesian Fathers have a theological seminary. The Monastery of Cremisan is renowned for the wine produced by its Salesian monks who run a farm. Nearby, the Salesian

The Seminary of Beit Jala

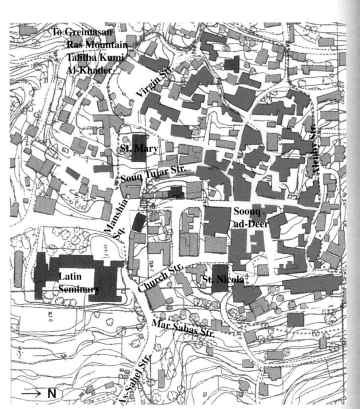

Beit Jala Historic Center. Unesco-PA Emergency Action Plan.

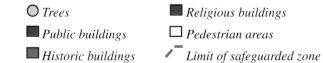

○ *Trees*	■ *Religious buildings*
■ *Public buildings*	□ *Pedestrian areas*
■ *Historic buildings*	╱ *Limit of safeguarded zone*

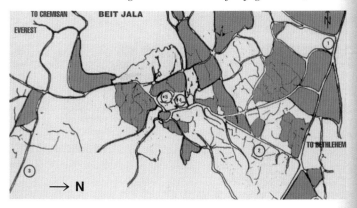

1) Rachel's Tomb.   *2) Hospital (al-Husien).*

3) Talitha Kumi School   *4) The Church of the Virgin.*

5) St. Nicolas Church.

Cremisan Convent

Sisters opened in 1859 their Noviciate for the Near East. At the top of the hill *(ar-Ras)*, a diverged road on the right leads to the Bethlehem Arab Society for Rehabilitation and to the Everest resort center. The view from the top of the hill is spectacular, with the greater part of Jerusalem visible. On the left, the road leads to Talitha Kumi Secondary School. The road from here leads to the Arab Muslim village of *al-Khader* (St. George). Due to the encroaching expansion of the Jewish suburb of Gilo, Beit Jala now borders Jerusalem. On the southern side is the small *'Ayda* refugee camp and Rachel's Tomb. Beit Jala has a perennial well, *Bir 'Ona*, and the people have a tradition that Mary rested there on her way from Bethlehem to 'Ain Karem.

The town has many schools and institutions, among the most important is *The Bethlehem Arab Society for Rehabilitation*, founded in 1960 as a home for the handicapped. Today a wide spectrum of services is given including intensive and comprehensive rehabilitation services for people with handicaps, through either its centralized community based day care centers or its out-reach programs.

In 1882, the Salesian Father Belloni, after founding the orphanage in Bethlehem in 1863, founded the Cremisan Convent to be the noviciate for the brothers and priests of the Holy Family. Since the beginning, Fr. Belloni intended to build a wine cellar in Cremisan as a source of income for the maintenance of the foundation. The wine cellar was started in 1885.

The entrance to Beit Jala

Beit Jala, General View

In 1977, modern equipment was added and the winery produces the famous Cremisan wine. Not far from the Convent, on the same road, there is a Vocational School and a Youth Center run by the Salisian Sisters.

Talitha Kumi Secondary School is a German institution with a boarding section for girls and a guest house for pilgrims. The school recently established a tourism program. There is also a Christian Cultural Center *Beit al-Liqa'* and the *Cultural Center of "Iskandar Khuri"*.

Talitha Kumi

From 1940 until the beginning of the Israeli occupation in 1967, Beit Jala was a beautiful summer resort frequented by tourists because of its good weather, attractive scenery, and its location on top of a mountain overlooking Jerusalem,

Bethlehem and other places. In the town there are several hotels where vacationers used to spend the hot summer months. The Everest resort lies on the top of Beit Jala's mountain (*930m.*) with a panoramic view of Jerusalem and Bethlehem. The resort provides entertainment facilities for children. The frequent use of Spanish among the inhabitants reveals the fact that large numbers have had connections with Latin America. Many migrate to South America from here.

Important Telephone Numbers

Arab Rehabilitation Society
Tel: 744050   Fax: 744053

Talitha Kumi Tourist Program
Tel: 744712 Fax: 741847
E-Mail: talitha@planet.edu

The Seminary of Beit Jala
Tel: 742612, 742885

Cremisan
Tel: 742355

Beit al-Liqa'
Tel & Fax: 050 480784

Al-Khader:
(St. George)

A short distance out of Beit Jala is the village of al-Khader, a little town of 5,000 inhabitants. It is surrounded by vineyards, fig and olive trees. It can be reached via Beit Jala or the Bethlehem-Hebron Road. The entrance to the village is marked

Christians and Muslims visit the monastic chapel

The stone gate

by a distinctive stone gate. Inside the village, there is the Greek Orthodox monastery of St. George (*Mar Giries or al-Khader*), a popular site of pilgrimage where the sick and insane are often brought to be cured by the so-called Chains of St.George. The first church in the monastery was established in 1600 A.D. on the site where St. George is believed to have lived a part of his life.

The present church was built in 1912 along with the convent and a mental hospital. The latter is not in use anymore but the monastery is still the source of a very rich store of religious folklore.

The Church is visited by many local people, especially on the Saint's day, May 5th. People present their votive offerings, such as candles, oil and sanctified loaves. During Turkish times, the rooms beside the Convent were used to house the mentally disturbed, and some believed that al-Khader would heal them. Thus al-Khader or St. George is one of the saints who is attributed with healing patients when their relatives appealed to him in piety to cure their loved ones.

St. George Monastery

Solomon's Pools

Al-Khader is also attributed with protection; hence, a sculpture

St. George Patron Saint of Christian Homes

of St.George killing the dragon decorates the façade of many Christian houses and a few Muslim ones in the district.

Open: 8.00 –12.00 a.m.
2.00 – 6.00 p.m.

Solomon's Pools:

Three pools surrounded by pine trees are located 5 kms (*3.1 miles*) south of Bethlehem on the road to Hebron and have been attributed to the prosperous period of King Solomon (*950 BC*) as mentioned in the Book of Ecclesiastics. *"I made me great works; I built me houses, and planted vineyards; I made gardens and orchards, and set them with trees of all kinds; and I made me ponds of water to water therewith the wood of the young trees".* King Solomon the Wise, as mentioned in the Bible, constructed these pools for his wives, reportedly one thousand in number, so that they could bathe here.

King Solomon

The Burak Castle

These pools were part of an ancient waterway supplying water to Jerusalem. They were repaired by Pontius Pilate. Herod the Great *(30 B.C.)* carried water by aqueduct from here to Herodium and probably to Jerusalem. Under the Turks, water from these pools reached Jerusalem by a four-inch clay pipe laid in 1902. Below the second pool are the pump station and pipes that took the water to the old city in Jerusalem. These pipelines replace two ancient aqueducts, the course of which can be traced on the way to Jerusalem. There is no doubt that both the Romans and Saracens made use of them and it is possible that the Roman reservoirs were enlargements or restorations of pools originally prepared by King Solomon. Today, this water is only used by inhabitants in the immediate vicinity.

The three large reservoirs, following each other in line, at a distance of 50 m. from each other, are partly excavated from the rock and partly built; they are intended to collect the rainwater that descends from the overlooking mountains and the water of the springs of the surrounding countryside. The length, width and depth of the three pools are respectively in meters: *179x64x15, 124x70x12, 116x70x8*. Near the Upper Pool stands a small Turkish castle, *El Burak*. It is a fortified *khan* of the 17th century now in a rather dilapidated condition. It was built by the Ottoman Sultan Suleiman the Magnificent in 1617. This rectangular fortress, flanked by a square tower at each of its angles and furnished with battlements, was built as barracks for the Tur-

Chapel of the Sealed Garden in Artas

Artas Folklore Center

kish soldiers selected to guard the Pools of Solomon and the commercial caravans between Jerusalem and Hebron.

A little distance to the west of this structure is the Sealed Fountain of Solomon which regulated and secured the constant supply of water for the Holy City. Candles or tapers are necessary when visiting it because a flight of twenty steps by which it is approached leads into a dark vaulted chamber. Today, the pools require restoration and rehabilitation. Access to the pools is from a side road off the main highway.

Artas:

A road passing the Pools leads down to the Village of Artas; the name is a corruption of the Latin word Hortus, meaning garden. Its ruins are possibly those of the ancient city *Etam*. To the southeast, there opens a small fertile valley whose luxuriant vegetation contrasts with the aridity of the surrounding mountains that en-

close it on all sides. This rich valley is the site of the Gardens of Solomon. It is probable that Solomon alludes to the gardens Hortus Conclusus when he speaks of his beloved in the Canticle of Canticles: *"My sister, my spouse, is a garden enclosed a fountain sealed up. The plants are a paradise of pomegranates"*. *(IV 12-13)*. According to Josephus, the Roman historian, King Solomon, escorted by his armed guards,

The Roman historian Josephus

used to go every day at dawn to enjoy the abundance of the running waters in the middle of the gardens.

On the southern side of the valley, opposite the village, stands the pretty convent and the graceful chapel of *The Sealed Garden*. It was erected by the Archbishop of Montevideo, Uruguay, in 1901, after obtaining the permission from the Turkish ruler at that time. This convent was built by two architects from Bethlehem. It is now occupied by the sisters of the Hortus Conclusus, who came from Montevideo to make their home in the country of Jesus. Donations are the main source of income for this convent which provides important social services including an orphanage to the surrounding community. In close proximity to the church are remains of a Crusader church, a Roman palace, several Roman mills, Roman channels and a spring.

An annual *Lettuce Festival* is organized in the village in April by the Artas Folklore Center, with popular dance and a tour of the village.

Prophet Elijah

Mar Elias Monastery

From Jerusalem to Bethlehem the ancient road passes by St. Karisthma, Mar Elias, Tantur, Rachel's Tomb, King David's Wells and Bethlehem. Mar Elias is located 4 kms (2.4 miles) to the north of Bethlehem, on the way to Jerusalem. This Greek Orthodox monastery dates back to the 11th century. Here we are told that

Mar Elias Monastery

the great prophet, Elijah, lay down under the shade of an olive tree, weary, hungry, and care-worn. He had to flee from the infamous Jezebel who was seeking vengeance after Elijah slaughtered the priests of Baal *(1 Kings 19:5)*. The name of the monastery is associated with Elijah. Such association is not, however, based on any authentic knowledge, and the name *Mar Elias* is derived from the founder of the monastery, the Greek bishop of Bethlehem who was buried here in 1345. The monastery was destroyed by an earthquake in the year 1160 A.D. but was rebuilt in the same year. Part of the Medieval monastery remains until this day.

Many miracles are attributed to Mar Elias. To this day, as in the past, many children are dedicated to Mar Elias. This saint is thought to respond to the requests of barren women and ailing children. He is the Patron Saint of the drivers on the road. The Monastery is a popular site for pilgrims and we can still witness a colorful annual pilgrimage. On the Saint's day (August 2nd), local Christians and Muslims go to Mar Elias to visit the monastic chapel and to join friends, family and neighbors on the grounds of the monastery, picnicking under the olive trees. Some people bring their sacrifices or gifts such as loaves of bread, bottles of oil and candles. They leave them before the icons and hand their loaves to a novice monk who in turn distributes bits of the sanctified bread after performing the divine rites. Also, on Christmas day, the patriarchs pause here to be received by the notables

The bench of Mr. Holman Hunt

of the area, before making their solemn entry into Bethlehem. Adjacent to the Monastery of *Mar Elias*, a bench bears engraved inscriptions from the bible in several languages. It was erected in 1900 by Mrs. Holman Hunt in memory of her husband, the great pre-Raphaelite painter who spent many years in Palestine, and near this spot painted his great religious pictures *The Light of the World* and *The Scapegoat*.

Open: 8.00-11.00 a.m. 13.00-17.00 p.m. Tel: 760966

Bir Qadismou:

Near the Orthodox Monastery of *Mar Elias*, about 5 kms (3.1 miles) from Bethlehem there is a cistern on the right

Bir Qadismou

side of the road. It is called *Bir Qadismou* or the *Well of the Magi*. The Arabic name is a corruption of the Greek word *Kathisma*, a place of rest. It is related that the Virgin Mary rested there on her way to Bethlehem. So, about the middle of the 5th century the *Ecclesia Kathismathis*, a church in honor of the Virgin Mother of God was erected on this spot. Near this Sanctuary the celebrated Abbot Theodosius dwelt for a time before beginning his great monastic foundations. A tradition says that this well never dries up. Also, it is related that the wise men, after leaving the presence of Herod, did not know where to go, and being weary from their journey, stopped to draw water; at that moment they saw a star reflected in the well. Their weariness left them, and they followed the star till they came to the place where the infant Jesus lay. To us it is only a reminder that Mary and Joseph, as well as the Magi, must have taken this route according to the Gospel narrative. Another legend is associated with the place: Mary had a vision here of two people one rejoicing in the birth of the Messiah and the other refusing to accept him.

Jroun-al-Humus
(Field of Grey Peas) :

It is a vast field near Mar Elias covered with innumerable small pebbles, which has always struck the imagination of the local residents and furnished a subject for one of those moral stories which abound in the East. "One day a man was sowing chick-peas in that field, when Mary (others say Jesus) passing by, asked him: "What are you sowing there, my friend?" "Stones", was the answer. "Very well, you will reap stones". And truly, when the sower came to gather them, he found nothing but petrified peas. From that time the Field of Grey Peas has been reminding passers-by of the punishment that follows a lie.

Opposite the field of Grey Peas is the Tantour Ecumenical Institute which was established in 1964 to promote understanding between Christian churches.

Tantur Ecumenical Institute

Monastery of St. Theodosius

THE DESERT MONASTERIES

During the latter half of the 5th century, the center of Christian monasticism shifted from Egypt to the Holy Land. Various centers were filled with scholars who were responsible for the spiritual revival of the period and played an important role in the development of the liturgy and dogma. Literature about the lives of the saints and stories of martyrs was recorded here. Monasticism evolved in these centers providing an important source for Christian inspiration throughout the centuries. The most prominent monastic centers lie to the east of Bethlehem in the Judaean wilderness. Bethlehem is the best departing point to visit the monasteries of St. Theodosius, St. Sabas and St. Chariton.

Monastery of St. Theodosius

Leaving Bethlehem by way of Beit Sahour, a road brings you to the imposing Greek Orthodox monastery of St. Theodosius in *al-Ubediyeh (10 kms, 6.2 miles)*. It is the largest and most highly-organized of these monasteries. According to tradition, the three Wise Men rested here after *"they were warned by God in a dream that they should not return to Herod; they departed into their country by another way" (Matt. 2:12)*. St. Theodosius, born in Cappadocia in 432, came to the cave where the wise men had stayed the night they left Bethlehem, and started the monastery in 476 which was the most populous convent with 693 monks. It contained four churches, and the services were given in four languages: Greek, Georgian, Armenian and Slavic. The Monastery was sacked in 808 A.D. and the monks abandoned the place.

During the Crusader period, religious life was established again in the Monastery and visitors in 1185 saw many towers. Many monks dwelt in cells; some of which were inacces-

St. Theodosius

sible caves reached only by ladders. Some led a life of silence and contemplation; these lived out of sight or sound of each other. Others were preoccupied in the intensive study of the Scriptures. Today, after fifteen centuries of unbroken history, the monastery still lives on. Eighteen steps bring you down to the cave where the remains of the founder, St. Theodosius rest in peace. He died in 529 at the great age of 105. In a cave recess, a cluster of skulls of anonymous monks can be seen, with crosses between their eye-sockets.

The present monastery was constructed by the Greek Orthodox Church at the turn of the century on the ruins of the Byzantine complex and incorporates the remains of an old Crusader building. The present church was completed in 1952. Around the church are visible remains of mosaic pavements, broken columns and capitals, but the greater part of the remains is under ground. From St. Theodosius, a good road leading down hill on the left, goes back to Jerusalem through *Abu Dis*. This road is used by the local people to reach *Ramallah* since the closure of Jerusalem by the Israelis. The road which runs straight on the mountain spine leads to Mar Sabas.

Bus # 60 runs from the Bus Station in Bethlehem to St. Theodosius. Ring for admittance to the convent. Open: 8.00 a.m.-1.00 p.m. Telephone 050-282447

Mar Sabas Monastery

Leaving the Monastery of St. Theodosius, the same route leads you to another Greek Orthodox monastery which lies 14.5 km *(9 miles)* east of Beth-

Mar Sabas Monastery

A view of the desert

lehem. It is one of the oldest inhabited monasteries in the world. Dating back to the 5th century, it was founded by Saint Sabas of Cappadocia. St. Sabas, who lived to be 94, exerted great influence on the emperors of his time, including Justinian. The monastery enjoyed imperial patronage during this formative period of monasticism. Mar Sabas died in the Monastery in 533 A.D., after having founded six monasteries and four hospices.

While driving on the road to the monastery of Mar Sabas in this wilderness, one has the irresistible feeling of stepping out of time. There is a stupendous view of the Desert of Judaea and the Dead Sea, backed by the Mountains of Moab. Suddenly the monastery with its girdle of walls and towers, comes into view. It is a unique structure, built in a highly individual way. The scene is so singularly wild, that verbal description can give little or no idea of it. This awe-inspiring complex, half-hidden in the Kidron Gorge, was an important place of pilgrimage even in the Crusaders' time.

The monastery is immense; it has 110 rooms, and few monks still dwell within its walls. It housed five thousand monks in its heyday. In the center of a paved courtyard, and in an octagonal domed chapel, St. Sabas was originally buried. His remains were transferred to Venice in 1256 by the Crusaders, but upon the request of Pope Paul VI, the bones were restored to their first resting place in 1965, at a time of rapprochement between the Catholic and Orthodox Churches. Today, the saint's body rests under an elaborately-sculptured canopy in the monastery's church. To the northwest is the Chapel of St. Nicholas, cut in the rock and the first church built by the Saint. Here can be seen scores of monks' skulls who suffered martyrdom at the hands of the Persians in 614. The chief memorial to the saint is his grotto, the *Lion's Grotto,* shown on the southern side of the monastery, near the guest chamber. In a rock fissure nearby is a palm tree, reputed to have been planted by St. Sabas. The dates which it bears, say the monks,

St. Sabas

have no pits. The rich library of St. Sabas is now in the Greek Patriarchate in Jerusalem.

Hundreds of icons cover the high walls of the monastery, but the richness of the painting fails to portray the austerity of its theme. One of the outstanding paintings is a representation of *the Day of Judgment*. Another depicts the burial of St. John of Damascus. Some of these icons have become legendary for their miracles. They are a living record of fifteen hundred years of ascetic and artistic production.

A visit to the Monastery may be concluded by a visit to the tomb of St. John of Damascus, a Greek theologian whose writings here in defense of the use of icons and the Orthodox faith were an important contribution to early Christianity. His remains were removed to Russia when the Russian church rebuilt the monastery in the early nineteenth century. The Canyon is dotted with cells and cave sepulchers. One of the most striking caves is that of Arcadios.

A visit to St. Sabas is not only an adventure but a true pilgrimage which recalls the most glorious era of the Eastern Church. Although Mar Sabas is reputed to have had a long tradition of hospitality to strangers, women have never been allowed to enter the ancient complex. However, as compensation, they may climb the specially constructed Women's Tower which offers tremendous views of this extraordinary medley of old buildings, to say nothing of the dramatic scenery of the gorge 180 meters below. Herman Melville, an American novelist, wrote a long poem of almost five thousand lines entitled Mar Saba in his famous book *Clarel: A Poem and Pilgrimage in the Holy Land* (1876). He wrote also another long poem about Bethlehem.

There is no bus service to Mar Sabas. You have to walk 5 kms (3.1 miles) from St. Theodosius. A round trip in a service taxi can be arranged for U.S.$25. Open: Sun-Thur. 8.00 a.m.-4.00 p.m. Tel: 6473135

Herodium:

Herodium is a fortress built by Herod the Great in memory of his victory over Antigonus in 42 B.C. It is located in the wilderness of the Judean desert, 6 km (3.7 miles) to the southeast of Bethlehem. It is a cone-shaped hill, partly artificial, rising out of the ground. It is also known as the *Mountain of the Franks*, or in Arabic *Jebel Fourdis,* (The Hill of Paradise). According to the Roman historian *Josephus,* King Herod wished to be buried in his summer

Herodium

palace at Herodium, at an altitude of 830 meters above sea level. Shortly after the Massacre of the Innocents, his body was borne 39 kilometers from Jericho for internment here. *Josephus,* describes the elaborate funeral procession that brought his body here from Jericho, but archaeological surveys have so far failed to discover his tomb. *Josephus* tells us that there were twin rounded hills in the form of a woman's breasts, and Herod cut one down and piled the rock and earth on the other. On the great mound thus produced he constructed a circular palace, adorned with towers, and reached by a marble staircase of which traces still exist. Down below, Herod laid out his pleasance, bringing water for the pools and fountains from the reservoirs of Solomon, the main Jerusalem water supply, some miles away. It was a tremendous undertaking, and typical of its creator. It has another interest too. It was the first example of what was later, in the days of the first Arab rulers, to become common, namely a sumptuous retreat, on the very edge of civilization or even beyond it, wherein the prince could escape from the cares of the court and the city. From the top, this strange tyrant king could look down on Bethlehem, the city whose infants he ordered to kill for fear of a future rival. This hill serves, however, as a permanent reminder of the Massacre of the Innocents and of this cruel, brutal tyrant. The fatigue from the ascent is made up for by the beauty of the landscape which one can contemplate from the summit. Bethlehem and Jerusalem are spread out to the north, in the other direction is the bare expanse of the Judaean Desert, with the Dead Sea beyond. You can often catch a glimpse of the Dead Sea to the east.

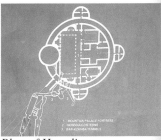

Plan of Herodium

Remains of the fortress

Recent excavations uncovered remains of a fortress: a double circular curtain wall with four towers and gateway from the north-east. Inside the walls were store rooms and water reservoirs. Remains of a hall with pillars and a bath house were found within the fortress. After the fall of Jerusalem in 70 A.D., the fortress was besieged and destroyed by the Romans. The lower Herodium area, at the foot of the mountain to the north, includes the remains of a fortress, store rooms, a hippodrome and a pool. Also, an aqueduct which brought water from Artas can be seen. Above this aqueduct, you can see some of the remaining steps which lead to the summit. In recent years, the remains of three Byzantine chapels with rich decorative mosaic floors show that the site continued to be inhabited during the fifth and sixth centuries. Later, the Crusaders *(or Franks)* made their final stand here before being ousted by the Muslims, giving the hill one of its alternative names, The Mountain of the Franks.

Herodium can be reached by a shared taxi service from Beit Sahour. A taxi from Bethlehem costs about $20 for a round trip.
Open: Sat-Thur: 8.00 a.m. - 17.00 p.m., Entrance: $US 5

Khureitun:

Such is the Arab name both of the cave and of the ravine in which it is situated. It is located 2 kms *(1.2 mile)* south-east of Herodium and near the village of *Tequ'a* in the Jerusalem desert. *Khureitun* is the ruin of the Laura of *Souka* founded about 330 by *St. Chariton*, and in which he died. It was named after him. We find in this place the cave in which the holy hermit spent the last years of his life. St. Chariton used a hanging cave as his own cell accessible only by a ladder. The cave was occupied by other hermits also at a later date. It is a naturel grotto of labyrinthic character. It contains seven chambers on

A view of the Dead Sea

different levels, each is connected with the other by passages, some of which are very narrow and low. The explorer may easily lose his way, he should either be provided with a long thread to be used as a clue, or, better still, with a guide. The cavern consists of a contious series of galleries and side-passages, which are sometimes so low as to be passable by creeping only, but sometimes expand into large chambers. One of the chambers looks like a great Cathedral. A short rock-passage leads into a spacious chamber, about 38 meters long, from which several side-passages diverge.

It was at the top of a cliff and near a spring. Near St. Chariton, a prehistoric grotto was found in 1928, with abundant materials of the Paleolithic period. Visitors are advised to come provided with a flashlight and a long rope if they wish to explore the different chambers of the cave. Also, they should take drinking water to avoid dehydration in the desert air and dress appropriately both for the monasteries and from the searing sun.

Tequ'a :

To the south-west of Herodium's Palace, about 3 kms (1.8 miles) south-west of the grotto of St. Chariton, and through an arid plain, lies Tequ'a, a Canaanite village. It is marked in the Madaba map, and is known through Crusaders' sources. This town, like Bethlehem, was an outpost towards the desert. Above all, it is distinguished as having been the birthplace of the prophet Amos, who, according to a tradition, is likewise buried here. Tequ'a used to be populously inhabited, and reportedly is the original home of numerous Bethlehemite families. Today, Tuqu'a is an Arab Muslim village, inhabited by 6,000 people. At present there are several artesian wells and pumps which pump water to all parts of the Bethlehem district, to Jerusalem and to other places.

Women carrying water from the wells of Tuqu'a

The village has the remains of several buildings, a church, water channels and column fragments. Its ruins are strewn far and wide over the broad top of one of the highest hills in the area. The view from it is magnificent. It is such a panorama as, once seen, can never be forgotten. On the west, the whole sweep of the range from Mizpeh to Hebron is visible. To the east lies the wilderness and the Dead Sea. Beyond the Sea and the Jordan is the unbroken chain of Moab and Gilead. To the north is Bethlehem. Below it, there is the wild ravine of Khureitun, in the bottom of which, at a distance of 3 km, is the Cave of Adullam. The cave has been regarded, by a monastic tradition reaching back to the time of the Crusaders, as the Adullam in which David took refuge after his romantic adventure at Gath *(Sam.xxii.1)*. To the southeast of Tequ'a there are many ancient sites, especially the ruins of the *New Laura*, founded in 508 by St. Sabas for rebel monks.

Among other main historical and archeological sites in the Bethlehem district are:

Abu Ghannaim (St Paul's Hill)
Beit Bassa
Battir
Bir al-Qutt
Husan
Nahhalin
Khirbet Jurish
Khirbet Kabar
Khirbet al-Mird
Um al-Qal'a
Umm Tuba

All can be reached by car.

Traditional Arts Museums & Handicrafts

The Old Bethlehem Home:

In 1970 the Women's Union restored the ground floor of their embroidery center in order to protect and house the embroidery collection and exhibit a variety of items that represent the Palestinian cultural heritage. The site was ideal as the house is located in an old quarter of Bethlehem, near the Church of Nativity. The house is one of the oldest types of architecture in town. Families were encouraged to donate their traditional belongings and the response to the campaign was spontaneous.

This house is called the *Old Bethlehem Home*. It contains different tools and items that were used in Bethlehem, in the 19th and the beginning of the 20th century. There also are several ancient pictures and documents related to the city. Five exhibition rooms contain the costumes and jewelry room,

the living room, the bedroom, the kitchen and the *taboun* (a traditional oven) which is located in the courtyard. There also are old photographs and a few display items in the corridors.

In the living room there is a *diwan* an arab ground-seat, covered with a carpet, as well as a bench covered with cushions and a carpet *Kilim.* The *hujrah,* a big red carpet striped with colors covers the floor. Under the carpet there is a mat made of straw *hasireh.* The altar: with icons, oil lamps and the special niche *ma'azil* for cotton mattresses and quilts are typical of the region.

In the Kitchen there are different items. The traditional kitchen utensils are made from different materials such as: pottery, wood, brass and straw. Most houses were provided with a stone hand-mill *Jarousha,* for grinding corn and dry cereals. Other utensils worth

Sitting and Bed Room

Part of the Kitchen

mentioning such as the pail (*dalu*) a vesel to pull water out of the cistern; and the iron-hook (*Khattafa*) consisting of a metal ring with attached hooks is used to pull out the pail when lost in the cistern.

In 1984, the *Old Bethlehem Home* was extended. An adjacent old house was bought and re-stored. This addition is one of the few authentic old houses left in Bethlehem. It might be similar to the house in which Jesus was born. The ground floor *al-Rawya* was the place

where sheep and goats were kept. On top of this room is *al-Sala* or the all-purpose room. The *Sala* or *Saloon* was used as a living room, a sitting room and a bedroom. Saint Joseph might have come to Bethlehem and stayed with Mary in such a

Local Embroidery

house. The Virgin would thus have given birth to Jesus in *al-Rawya,* since it was the only private room. Finally, there is *al-Illiya.* The *al-Illiya* depicts the lifestyle of Bethlehemites between 1900-1932.

A small showroom upstairs sells gorgeous examples of local

Jacket worn over the Dress

Traditional Handicrafts

hand-embroidered items such as cushions, runners, table clothes, handbags, etc. at a reasonable price. These items are made at home by Palestinian women.

In addition to the *Old Bethlehem Home*, the Union has begun constructing of a second museum, a 1000 square meter structure made of stone. It is being built around a Roman aqueduct uncovered for about ten meters; this will be a special attraction for visitors. The new museum is located on the Hebron road and will be for tourists. It will be opened as a living museum and will house a permanent collection of contemporary painting, sculpture, furniture and objects of art. The building also will have rooms dedicated to workshops in pottery, olive wood, Mother-of-Pearl, straw crafts and cooking.

Open: Monday to Saturday: 10:00 - 1200 a.m. & 14:30 - 17:00 p.m.
Entrance: US $1 per person.
Tel: 742453

The Folklore Museum of Beit Sahour:

The Beit Sahour Folklore Museum is located in the town center near the Municipality. It was founded in 1991 by citizens of Beit Sahour supported by the municipality in order to collect, preserve and depict the cultural heritage of the country, the daily life styles, customs and traditions. Included are household objects for preparing food, coffee, tea and bread; musical instruments; old arms and saddles; objects used in religious rituals. Also, there are models of traditional handicrafts made of different materials in-

The new building

Beit Sahour Folklore Museum

cluding straw, needle work, pottery, wool, hay, olive wood and Mother-of-Pearl.

The emphasis of the Folklore Museum is on the peasant's life, exhibiting a sampling of the folk artifacts and crafts, representing scenes of every day life. For example, there is an exhibit showing a peasant wedding ceremony in all its details, and a collection of costumes from different parts of Palestine, as well as agricultural tools and handicrafts.

The displays are in three different halls according to objective sequences; some are presented in showcases, some are displayed in the open air. They date back to the 19th and the beginning of the 20th century.

In addition, the museum has his own folklore group that holds outdoor festivals including dances and representation of a Palestinian wedding.

Open: Monday to Saturday 8.00 a.m. to 1.00 p.m. P.O.Box 56, Beit Sahour. Tel: 6473666

Traditional dress

The Folklore Group

Center for Palestinian Traditional Costumes:

This Center aims at modernizing and marketing the traditional costumes of Palestinian women. It produces embroidered and ornamented traditional dresses, handkerchiefs, bed covers and other items for use in houses and offices. In addition to sale items, there are others for display. The center includes a Palestinian tent and displays various tools used in the old days and traditional dresses from various periods with explanations of each. Visitors and tourists may have their photos taken while in Palestinian traditional dresses.

Location: Manger Street, behind Saca Brothers Souvenir Shop. Open: Monday to Saturday 11:00 - 19:00 p.m. Tel & Fax: 742642. P.O.B. 146, Bethlehem.

Olive Wood Crafts:

The manufacture of religious articles and souvenirs from olive wood is not only traditional in the district of Bethlehem but the products are internationally known. It is believed that the craft was begun in Bethlehem in the fourth century following the construction of the Church of the Nativity at which time the monks taught the craft to the local residents. The origins of this craft are obscure, but one of the earliest products were rosary beads carved from olive pits.

Because of religious associations with the olive tree and because of the availability of supplies of wood, wood carving has been very popular. This craft is one of the few profes-

Olive wood: Nativity Set

sions to be passed down through generations. It later spread to surrounding towns, mainly Beit Jala and Beit Sahour which are

Palestinian Traditional Costumes: Maha Saca's Collection

Olive Wood Factory

part of the Bethlehem area. Olive wood carving is the most important tourist craft in Bethlehem. A number of superb artists continue this tradition.

Wood carving is the process of shaping wood into decorative and sculptural forms. Olive wood is used because it can be worked readily and accurately with simple hand tools. Also, it has a nice variety of natural color and tonal depth, due to the annular structure. It is also resistant to decay and receptive to a number of surfacing treatments. Rough cutting is done on machines programmed with the master design model. The finest work incorporating facial expressions and intricate details, must be chiseled by hand. After sanding, the items are machine buffed with

Olive wood: biblical statuettes

Olive wood: The Nativity Scene

homemade clothes permeated with beeswax. This is the only finish they require. Varnish is avoided because it will eventually cause the olive wood to crack.

Olive wood rosaries and crosses

Over one thousand different gift items are made from olive wood like boxes, picture frames, covers for historical and old books, candle holders, rosaries, urns, vases and Christmas ornaments. Olive wood is crafted into crèche scenes with individual figures of Jesus, Mary, Joseph, the three Magi, the shepherds and even cows and sheep. Often these are enclosed in an open-sided stable surrounded by palm trees. Above them hovers a shooting star. *Beit Art Center* that sponsors the

traditional crafts of the Holy Land was established in 1989 under the auspices of the Latin Patriarchate of Jerusalem to initiate income generating projects to help support the local community. It's first project target was the olive wood carving industry characteristic of the Bethlehem area.

Mother-of-Pearl:

Franciscan Friars from Damascus are credited with establishing the craft in Bethlehem between the 14th and the 16th centuries. To teach local residents, they brought in craftsmen from Genova. Initially artisans used Mother-of-Pearl coming from the Red Sea. Today, abalone shells come to Bethlehem from Australia, California, Mexico, Brazil and New Zealand. Because of its thickness, it is possible to carve relief in the shells. The mother-of-pearl is taken from the rest of the shell and pieces are used for mosaics. Experienced workers use the mother-of-pearl to create delicate filigrees. Most popular items are crosses, ear-

Mother-of-Pearl Factory

rings and brooches. In cheaper items, plastic is interwoven with mother-of-pearl. However, plastic lacks the multihues of so called white mother-of-pearl.

A Mother-of-Pearl Nativity Set

The Bethlehem area includes 63 olive wood and 56 mother-of-pearl workshops. Nevertheless, local predictions are that mother-of-pearl carving will soon belong to Bethlehem's history because the work requires intense concentration and highly skilled craftsmanship. Shimmering colors and lace-like carvings may end up only in museums.

Embroidery :

Traditional women costumes in Palestine, the origin of which goes back more than four thousand years, are still much in use in the area, especially in

Palestinian woman embroidering

nearby villages. They are distinguished mainly by using embroidery and needle work, which has fascinated women both in the Orient and the West. Hand embroidery is a special trade mark in Bethlehem.

Tourists frequently buy such costumes, or such items as embroidered handkerchiefs, bed covers, runners, table cloth and the like. High prices are normally paid because of the skill and time involved. In the streets and the crowded market, it is possible to see women with high heels, a belted waist with a large bodice embroidered

A Chest Panel

Accessories worn by Bethlehem Arab Women

with gaily-colored flowers, and a white veil flowing down to the shoulders.

The main garment is a flowing dress, and a special head-cover. The *Qabbeh* (chest-panel) was embroidered with golden and silk threads, in various geometrical designs. On the sleeves and on both sides of the dress were triangular pieces embroidered in bright red or green.

The *Shatweh* (head dress) was another important element of a married woman's dress. It was made of several layers of embroidered material, to which was added coral beads, golden and silver coins. Over the *Shatweh* a *tarbi'a* (veil) was placed to cover the shoulders and a part of the back. This form of head dress echoes those worn by medieval western women. The style arrived in Palestine at the time of the Crusaders.

Around the waist, a Cashmere or woolen shawl was generally tied as a belt, and a short jacket, *taksireh* was worn over the dress. This was embroidered with silk for everyday use, but with golden or silver threads for feasts or special occasions. In winter, women put on a short woven woolen overcoat striped in red and black.

The beauty of such clothes is enhanced by red leather shoes. For everyday life, women turn the pointed sleeves and tie them in the back, enabling them to carry on with their everyday work. These simple garments were embroidered with various colored threads in cross stitch.

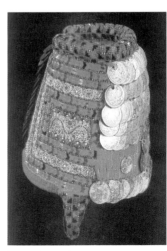

The Shatwah

Palestinian Cuisine and Food:

Bethlehem is worth visiting for its houses of worship, climate, and good food. A time comes when a visitor or tourist must eat. The Palestinian food is generally inexpensive and nutritious. Vegetarians will find a large number of delicious meat-free dishes. The least expensive option is street food and the smaller restaurants which specialize in one dish or type of dish, such as *hummus*, *fuul*, *falafel*, chicken *shawerma* and *kebab*. Other larger restaurants will serve fuller meals beginning with *mezze* (salads) and followed by a meat dish. Today there are also a number of more internationally focused restaurants and cafes. The price of a meal might range from US $5 in the least expensive places to US $30 in a fancy restaurant.

To write about Palestinian food is to describe Middle Eastern food. For all their diversity, Greece, Turkey, Lebanon, Syria, Jordan, Iraq, Palestine, Israel, Iran (Persia) and Egypt make a unified culinary world of their own.

The Arabic names of the dishes vary a little from one

Palestinian Food

country or another. Some ingredients such as pork, alcoholic or fermented liquids and all inebriating liquors are forbidden according to Muslim dietary laws. These similarities have remained in spite of the geographical, religious, cultural and political differences.

General Features of the Palestinian Food:

❦ *Cooking fat.* Samna (clarified butter) is the basic cooking fat. It can be replaced by ordinary butter, margarine and corn oil. Virgin olive oil is used in dishes to be eaten cold or raw such as salads.

❦ *Flavor & Aroma.* A large variety of spices are used to add flavor or aroma such as cumin, cinnamon, ginger, mastic, black pepper, allspice, sumac, saffron, cardamom and coriander (dry or fresh). These are added to various dishes and drinks for color and taste. Also, parsley, mint, garlic, onion are abundantly used .

❦ *Lemony Flavor.* Cooked yogurt, sumac, vinegar, lemon, pomegranates, tamarind and tomatoes give the lemony flavor. Some of these can be used interchangeably.

❦ *Meat.* Lamb is the basic meat in most dishes. Beef comes next. Chicken and squab meat are widely used in a variety of dishes.

❦ *Bread & Rice.* Wheat bread, pitta bread, *shrak*, and *manaquish bil-za'tar* (flat bread baked with olive oil and thyme) are basic sources of carbohydrate. Rice that comes in long or short grain is a basic component of most main dishes.

❦ *Vegetables.* Eggplant is a favorite vegetable. Zucchini is another.

❦ *Dairy products.* Yogurt is the preferred form of milk. Fresh yogurt is served with main dishes. It is used as a cooking liquid to provide sour flavor.

Popular Palestinian Food:
Mezze.

This is served with beer or 'Araq and can be a great delight and suitable to the Western way of life. A small assort-

Popular Food: olive, tomatoes, onion, bread, olive oil and thyme

ment of salads can be served with drinks as appetizers or *hors d'œuvre* dishes. A wider choice provides an exciting buffet dinner. Mezze includes nuts of all types, olives, cucumbers, tomatoes, cheese, boiled eggs or *Egga (*omelet-like*),* pickles, sauces or dips made with *tahina* (sesame paste), and these are usually served with little pieces of Arab bread, pitta. Mezze may also include the following:

• *Felafel:* These are patties made from ground dried chick peas, deep fried and served in a fresh pitta bread sandwich with salad, pickles, chips etc. Falafel can also be purchased separately. These patties are round but can be finger shaped and stuffed with onion and sumac.

• *Humus bi Tahina* (Chick peas with *tahina*): A smooth paste of chickpeas, tahina, spices, garlic, lemon and olive oil. This can be served with *Falafel* or meat or as one salad in a *mezze*.

• *Fuul*: Stewed fava beans, mashed with a fork and served warm with lemon, garlic and olive oil.

• *Baba Ghanouj* (Aubergine or eggplant with *tahina*): Baked or grilled aubergine, mashed with a fork and mixed with tahina, lemon, salt, garlic and olive oil.

• *Salata Turkiya*: Spiced salad of tomato paste, hot pepper puree, parsley and onion.

• *Labanah*: a delightful cream cheese, made by salting yogurt and allowing it to drain overnight in a fine cotton cloth. It can be served alone with olive oil or with green olive or with cucumber.

• *Tabbouleh* or *Burghul Salad*: Cracked wheat, mixed with chopped parsley, mint, onions, tomato, cucumber, olive oil and lemon. It should be lemony.

• *Baqdounsia:* Tahina cream salad with finely chopped parsley.

• *Zeitoun:* green and black olives, plain or stuffed with hot pepper.

• *Shawerma*: Paper-thin slices of crisp roast lamb meat, beef or turkey, cooked on one large skewer. It is usually served in pitta bread with a variety of salads, mainly onion and sumac, *tahina* cream salad and pickles or as a main course with *hummus bi tahina* and other salads.

• *Kebab* or *Kofta* (grilled minced meat on skewers): Served on a plate with finely chopped onions, parsley and salad or in a pitta bread sandwich. Lamb is the preferred meat, but beef or a mixture of both can be used.

• *Kubbeh*: Minced meat cooked with onion and encased in cracked wheat. It is served either raw, grilled or fried.

• *Sambousek:* A half-moon shaped pie stuffed with meat filling or cheese filling. It could be three-cornered pie stuffed with spinach.

• *Sfeeha*: A type of pizza with a minced meat topping which contains chopped tomatoes, green pepper, onions and parsley.

Main Meals:

• *Farrouj Mahshi:* Chicken stuffed with spiced rice and

meat, roasted in the oven, and served with yogurt or vegetables.

• *Musakhan*: Grilled chicken, served on a bed of sautéed onion and sumac. All are placed on fresh Arab bread.

• *Maqlubeh*: Layers of rice, fried meat and vegetables (aubergine and cauliflower) cooked in a pan and served upside down.

• *Mujadara*: Rice cooked with lentils and onions.

• *Kusa Mahshi*: Courgettes or zucchini stuffed with rice and meat. Eggplant, tomatoes, potatoes and green pepper can be stuffed, too.

• *Waraq Dawali*. Stuffed vine leaves with rice and meat. Meat can be replaced by onion, garlic, tomato, parsley and dried mint.

• *Waraq Malfuf:* Cabbage leaves stuffed with rice and meat.

• *Mulokhia*: Stewed vegetable something like spinach, served with rice dishes, lamb meat or chicken. Egyptians prefer rabbit meat.

• *Kidra*: Saffron rice and lamb meat, sprinkled with all spices, cardamom and garlic. Cooked in a traditional oven and in a special pot, served with yogurt.

• *Mansaf (*a yogurt like food*)*: Cooked and seasoned rice spread on flat baked *shrak (*a whole wheat crust*)*. Boiled lamb meat is piled on top of the rice. Before eating, yogurt soup is poured over the rice and meat, and fried pine nuts are sprinkled for both flavor and decoration.

• *Meshwi* (Grills): All types of meat, large or small pieces, grilled or roasted over a fire, served with plain rice, salads and pitta or Arab bread.

NB. Most of the above dishes require time and craftsmanship. Preparation and cooking are slow and lengthy. Therefore it is preferable to contact the restaurant ahead of time to examine the possibility of having any of these dishes. Few hours would be enough for a small group while 1 or 2 days would be needed for a large group.

Fruits in the Market Place in Bethlehem

Desserts and Pastries:

Following the main dish, fresh fruit (according to the season) is served as dessert. Melons, citrus fruit, bananas, apples, grapes and prunes are best examples. A good meal ends with a cup of coffee served with local pastries. They are usually sweet, made from semolina, butter, flour, nuts, cheese, soaked in rich sugar syrup.

- *Kenafeh*: Soft cheese cooked between two layers of orange shredded pastry, served with "Qatter" (sugar syrup with rose water).
- *Baklawa*: Pastry layers with nuts and syrup.
- *Qatayef*: Pancakes stuffed with chopped walnuts, sugar and cinnamon or cheese; soused with syrup. They are specialty for the Muslim feast of Ramadan.
- *Ma'mul*: Little stuffed pastries (semolina dough) with different shapes and fillings: walnuts, pistachios, almond or dates, rolled in powdered sugar. They are an Easter specialty.
- *Hilbah*: A flat dough prepared with Semolina, olive oil, and fenugreek seeds. Baked either plain (one layer) or stuffed with nuts filling (in the center of two layers) and served with syrup.
- *Ghoraybeh*: Plain pastries made of butter, flour and sugar. They come in different shapes: S shape, fingers or bracelets.

Drinks & Beverages :

Qahwa: Arabic coffee mixed with ground cardamom, boiled and served with or without sugar, according to taste and occasion.

Shay: Tea with mint, or sage

leaves which give a special flavor. *Shay bi na'na*: Mint tea *Shay bi maramia*: Tea with sage
- *Lemonada*: Soft drink usually served cold, made from lemon or orange syrup.
- *Tamar hindi*: Sweet, heavy tamarind juice.
- Sahlab: Sweet hot milk, served with coconut, raisins and cinnamon.

Local Alcoholic drinks:
- *Araq*: An aniseed flavored spirits; drunk alone, or with ice cubes or water which turns it milky.
- *Taybeh:* The first Palestinian beer, made in the German style in the Taybeh micro brewery.
- *Wine:* from the vineyards of the monasteries of Cremisan or Latrun.

Restaurants

Restaurants in Bethlehem offer a variety of traditional, and international food. Fast food including *falafel*, *pizza*, hamburger and *shawerma* can be

Nativity Hotel Restaurant

121

obtained for US$3 to 5 per person, while a complete menu with aperitif, dessert, and beverage is about US $20 to 25 per person. The following is a list of restaurants in Bethlehem arranged according to location.

Manger Square

Al-Andalus
Tel: 743519
Eastern & Western food
St. George
Tel: 743780
Eastern & Western food

Milk Grotto Street

Al-Ameer
Tel: 742783
Eastern & Western food

Manger Street

Dolphine
Tel: 743432, Sea food
Mundo
Tel: 741961
Fast food & Ice-cream
Abu Shanab
Tel: 742985, Eastern food
Nisan
*Panoramic view &
luxurious interior*
Tel: 741248, 741249.
Fax: 6470456
Eastern & Western food.

Sababa
Tel: 744006, Eastern food
Hamburger House
Tel: 741064
Hamburger, Hot-Dogs
& Shawerma.
Pastry King
Tel: 6470077, 741458
Eastern pastries.
Dollar
Tel: 744007, Eastern food
Al-Diwan
Tel: 740333, Fast Food

Hebron - Jerusalem Road

Al-Karawan
Tel: 747439, Eastern food
Baloons
Tel: 741036
Italian food & Ice cream.
Central
Tel: 744404, 741378
Eastern food
Kleopatra
(Restaurant & Disco)
Tel: 741961, Eastern &
Western food (*Self Service*)
Philadelphia
Tel: 745450, Eastern food
Tatchi the Chinese
Tel: 744382, Chinese food
Bugs Bunny, *Coffee Shop*
Tel: 6470596, Fried Chicken
Samer
Tel: 742317
Eastern & Western food

Nissan Restaurant

Nissan Restaurant is equipped to serve 1000 people.

Cinema Square.

Dalila
Qarra'a Building
Tel: 743634
Eastern & Western food
Horse Shoe
Madbassa Street
Tel: 742287
Fast food & Ice-cream
Shepherd
(Hotel and Restaurant)
Naser Street, Tel: 740656
Eastern & Western food
Abu Fouad
Paul VI St. Tel: 743229
Traditional fast food
Al-Manqal
Nasser St. Tel: 6470896
Eastern food & Fast food

Beit Jala

Barbra Restaurant
Arab Society Road, Tel: 744578
Eastern food (*Panoramic view*)
Everest
Tel: 742604, 741278
Eastern food
San Rock Restaurant
Tel: 743128, 050 307256
Al-Sahel St. Eastern &
Western food
El Pollo Chicken Restaurant
Al-Sahel St. Tel: 742373
Orthodox Club Restaurant
Tel: 745097, Western Food

Beit Sahour

Happy Days
Y.M.C.A. Street,
Tel: 050 470532
Fast food
Muntazah al-Khiam
Ar-Ra'wat Street,
Eastern food (outdoor)
Muntazah Beit Sahour
(indoor and outdoor)
Tel: 647 3023, Eastern food.

Bethlehem District:

The Bethlehem district includes within its boundaries 3 major towns: Bethlehem, Beit Jala and Beit Sahour, 71 Palestinian towns and villages such as el-Khader, el-'Ubaydiyah, Artas, Beit Fajjar, Dar Salah, Marah Rabah, Nahaleen, Tequ'a, Wadi Fukin, Umm Salamuna, Za'tara, 3 refugee camps: 'Aida, Daheisheh, Beit-Jebren, and 20 Israeli settlements. The district's total population is estimated at 132,460 Palestinians representing 5.7% of the total population of the Palestinian Territories. This number includes 13,451 people living in the above refugee camps. Out of the total population 64,291 people are living in rural areas.

Christians and Muslims: good neighbours…

	Inhabitants	Christians in %	Moslems in %
Bethlehem	40.000	38	62
Beit Sahour	14.000	83	17
Beit Jala	14.800	86	14

Muslims constitute 67% of the district and the remaining 33% are Christians. Christians constitute the majority only in the two towns of Beit Jala and Beit Sahour. Among Christians, the Orthodox denomination is the largest. Although Christians have traditionally been the majority of the population of Bethlehem City, their number have been reduced in the last 28 years. Presently Muslims represent the majority of the population with 62 %. Such demographic change is a result of Christian immigration to other countries and Muslims emigration from rural areas, and nearby villages and refugee camps. Owing to several cruel events that befell the region, since the beginning of the century, many of its inhabitants had emigrated to South America and other places. There are 300,000 immigrants from the Bethlehem area in Chile.

Economy:

Tourism and its related enterprises form a major industry in the region. They play a crucial role in developing the local economy. More than 20% of the working population are employed in the tourism sector. Pilgrims come to Bethlehem all year around with the low season during the winter months from November to February. However, Christmas is the high point. More than two million tourists and pilgrims visit the birthplace of Jesus every year. In fact, a trip to the Holy Land without a visit to Bethlehem is just unthinkable. Today, it is one of the world's most celebrated religious places. Indeed long before the age of modern tourism, the town was one of the star attractions of the Middle East. It has been welcoming visitors from around the word ever since.

The people of Bethlehem have developed high quality artisan craftsmanship mainly Mother-of-Pearl, Olive Wood, religious and secular items. The town owes much of its property to the manufacture of religious objects made from Olive Wood, Mother-of-Pearl and coral. Over one thousand different gift items are made and sold mainly to pilgrims and tourists. Hand embroidery is another special trade mark in Bethlehem. Other industries include textile, chemical and stone manufacturing. Bethlehem has a long tradition of skilled stonemasons, working the high quality stone that

Distribution of Palestinian Communities in the West Bank & Gaza

Community	Number	Population
District cities	4	25 %
Other cities	9	14 %
Small Towns	50	19 %
Villages	70	10 %
Small Villages	376	15 %
Refugee Camps	28	17 %

comes from quarries in the vicinity of the town.

Travel & Tourist Agencies in Bethlehem

Crown Tours	2-740911
Gloria	2-743021
Joy International	2-6470330
King David	2-6470054
Lama Tours	2-742847
The Nativity	2-742966
Kukali Tours	2-6472034

Airline Companies
(in Jerusalem):

Air France	02-282535
Alitalia	02-283515
British Airways	02-288654
KLM	02-284896
Scandinavian	02-287238
Olympics	02-9953538
Sabena	02-9952180

Education:

Education is compulsory for nine years. The district has 75 public schools and 19 private schools. These educational institutions are operated by either the government, private organizations (mainly churches), and the UNRWA. In Bethlehem private schools are dominant. After completing 12 years of school and passing the Tawjihi examination, students may attend a university in their country or aborad.

Bethlehem University:

Bethlehem University is one of the leading institutions for higher education in Palestine. It was founded in 1973, with the administrative cooperation of the De La Salle Brothers and the Vatican. It was established after the visit of Pope Paul VI to the Holy Land in 1964. During this visit, his holiness called for the foundation of new institutions to improve the quality of life for the people of the area. One of the specific priorities cited was a university for young Palestinians in their homeland. Bethlehem University offers Baccalaureate degrees in accounting, Arabic, biology, business administration, chemistry, elementary education, English, mathematics, nursing, physics, physiotherapy, sociology and social work. Diplomas are granted in clinical supervision, elementary education, hotel management, midwifery, pilgrim tour guiding, pre-school education, religious education, secondary education, tourism and travel agency management.

The main building of the University, constructed in 1893,

Bethlehem University

Tourism for Peace Program's Satellite Antenna

houses the general administrative offices and most of the Faculty of Arts. A chapel annex was built in 1907. The Library, dedicated in 1978, houses about 60,000 volumes and includes a special collection of microfiche and microfilm on the Middle East, and a Palestinian collection.

The Science Building, opened in 1980, contains laboratories and classrooms and a computer center. The Social and Cultural Center, dedicated in 1991, contains a cafeteria, assembly hall, offices and rooms for art, music, physical fitness and athletics. A residence for the Christian Brothers is on campus. The Mar Andrea Women's Hostel located off-campus, was completed in 1979; on the same property is a convent to house religious women who teach at the University.

Bethlehem University has grown from an initial enrollment of 78 students to some 2200, well over half of whom are women. The University has been frequently closed down by the Israeli authorities after demonstrations against the occupation. It is a short walk up the hill from Hebron road.

Al-Quds Open University

Established in 1985, the University applies an Open and Distance Learning System. The language of study is Arabic and the University applies a credit hour system where the scholastic year consists of two main semesters and a summer session. Every student may register between two and twenty one credit hours per semester. The University awards the first university degree in Agriculture, Social and Family Development, Applied Science and Technology, Management & Enterpreneurship and Education.

Bethlehem Bible College:

Founded in 1979, the Bible College provides training for Palestinians and other Christians wanting to become teachers, pastors, educators, church workers, evangelists, tour guides and administrators. The tour guide program helps train and provide licensed and qualified guides in anticipation of the increasing influx of tourists. The classes are conducted in Arabic. The summer Foreign Students Studies Program is conducted in English. The college accepts students from all denominations and offers courses from an outstanding faculty who combine high academic standards and deep spiritual commitment. Community Education Courses are offered for adults in the Bethlehem area.

The International Center of Bethlehem:

The International Center is a

The International Center

church-related organization. Its work is directed towards building a civil society and a sustainable economic development, and taking the Palestinian cultural heritage into consideration. The main programs are: women's studies, international relations, adult education, alternative tourism and German-Palestinian Exchange. The Center offers modern facilities that are ideal for holding seminars, lectures, and conferences.

Adjacent to the center is the Abu Gubran Guest House, which offers the opportunity to experience and enjoy the finest Arabic hospitality and to become acquainted with the beliefs and culture of the people of the Holy Land. Through the International Center of Bethlehem and the Abu-Gubran Guest House, people of all ages and cultures can participate in such cultural activities as the arts, music and literature, as well as the German and Arabic language courses.

Al-Lika' Center for Heritage & Religious Studies in the Holy Land:

The Center is located at the entrance of Bethlehem, near Rachel's Tomb. It is a place of research and study on the religious traditions and institutions of the people of the Holy Land and the region. The program includes annual conferences, interfaith dialogues, Palestinian contextualized theology in the Holy Land, international activities and the publication of *al-Lika' Journal*, a newsletter, books and occasional papers.

Tantur:

Tantur is Arabic for hilltop. A chapel and a hospital, supported by the Latin Order of St. John, were seen on the hill-top from 1846 until 1964. After the Pope's 1964 pilgrimage to the Holy Land, the Vatican purchased the Tantur terrain, then leased it to an ecumenical board to establish an international ecumenical institute for theological research and pastoral studies. The primary concern of Tantur continues to be the promotion of inter confessional and intercultural dialogue through advanced study and research. Resident junior and senior scholars do independent research or work with others on a major theme in biblical, historical, liturgical and theological studies. The Institute house a large and impressive library of 75.000 vols. and a Biblical Garden.

Tantur

The Biblical Garden

Tel: 6760911, Fax: 6760914, Hebron-Jerusalem Road at Gilo, junction. Buses 22,47 from Bethlehem.

List of Libraries in Bethlehem

1. Bethlehem University Library
Frères Street, P.O.B. 9,
Tel: 741243, Fax: 744440
Hours: Mon-Fri: 8.00-16.00
Open to the public on request. 60,000 vols. Academic collection, mainly in Arabic and English. Special collections include a Palestinian division and an audio-visual center.

2. Bethlehem Bible College
Hebron Road, P.O.B. 127
Hours: Mon-Fri 8.00-16.00
Sat: 8.00-12.00. 15,000 vols.
Christian books, Arabic, English. Tel: 741190, Fax: 743278

3. Pontifical Mission Library
Frères Street (Beside Bethlehem University). Hours: Mon-Fri: 9:00-12:00, 1:30-16:30. 30,000 vols. General collection in Arabic, English, French, Spanish. Videotheque (also in Arabic). Tel: 743077, Fax: 743077.

4. Studio Teologico Salesiano "S. Paolo"
Bethlehem, Cremisan, P.O.B. 160
Hours: Mon-Sat: 8.00-12.00, 14.30-18.30. 6,000 vols.
Philosophical, theological, biblical material etc. Italian, French, English, Arabic, 1000 scientific periodicals.
Tel: 742605,
Fax: 742847

5. Latin Patriarchate Seminary Library.
Open to the public on request. 30,000 vols. Collection in Arabic, French, English and Italian. Philosophical and theological material. Tel: 742612,
742885.

6. The Ecumenical Institute for Theological Studies.
75,000 vols.
Hours: 8:00-12:00 a.m.,
2:00-4:00 p.m.
Tel: 6760911,
Fax: 6760914.

Christian Schools in Bethlehem Area

Bethlehem

1- Syrian Catholic School, Manger Street. P.O.B. 199, Tel: 742497, Fax: 740334, Kg.

2- Terra Sancta High School, P.O.B. 92, Tel: 742237, Fax: 6470314, Kg. El. Prep. Sec.

3- College des Frères, Abdel Nasser Street, P.O.B. 261, Tel: 743244, Fax: 743244, Kg. El. Prep, Sec.

4- Don Bosco Salesian Technical School, Paul VI Street. P.O.B. 41, Tel: 742421, Fax: 747162, Technical, Secondary

5- Terra Santa Girls' School, Star Street, P.O.B. 65, Tel: 742680, Kg, El, Prep. Sec.

6- Rosary Sisters' School, Star Street, Tel: 742682, Kg. El.

7- Mar Afram, P.O.B. 1010, Tel: 744757, Kg.

8- Ev. Lutheran School, Madbaseh Street, P.O.B. 73, Tel: 744245, Fax: 744245, Kg. El. Prep.

Beit Sahour

1- Latin Patriarchate School P.O.B. 22, Tel: 6472278, Kg. El. Prep.

2- Greek Catholic Patriarchal School, P.O.B. 63, Bishop Abu Sa'ada Street, Tel: 6472424, Fax: 742424, Kg. El. Prep. Sec.

3- Evangelical Lutheran School, P.O.B. 55, Tel: 6472720, Fax: 6472204, Kg. El. Prep. Sec.

4- Greek Orthodox Secondary School. Tel: 647 2042, Kg. El. Prep. Sec.

Beit Jala

1- Latin Patriarchate School, P.O.B. 3, Tel: 742624, Fax: 742612, Kg. El. Prep. Sec.

2- Ev. Lutheran School Talitha Kumi, P.O.B. 7, Talitha Kumi Street, Tel: 741247, Fax: 741847, E-mail: talitha@planet.edu

3- Hope Secondary School, P.O.B. 5, Tel: 742268, Fax: 744332, Prep. Sec.

College des Frères

Educational Institutions:

1.Bethlehem University:
Tel: 741243, Fax: 744440
Email:
Webmaster@bethlehem.edu

2. Bethlehem Bible college:
Tel: 741190, Fax: 743278.
Email:
100320.3455@compuserve.com

3. The International Center of Bethlehem
Tel: 647 0047, Fax: 6470048.
Email:
annadwa@planet.edu

4. Tantur Ecumenical Institute
Tel: 676 0911, Fax: 6760914

5. The Pontifical Mission Library: Tel: 743077

6. The Open University:
Tel: 747387, Fax: 747388

7. The Salisian Industrial College: Tel: 742421

8. Al-Lika' Center :
Telfax: 741639

Climate:

The climate of Bethlehem for the greater part of the year is pleasant. Winter lasts for three months, from mid-December to mid-March, and can be severe. During the remainder of the year, the climate is temperate, with the hottest weather in the months of July and August.

Bethlehem district is characterized by great variation in its topography and altitude. The highest elevation of approximately 900 m above sea level is found in the Beit Jala area in the west. The eastern parts of the town are characterized by sharp slopes where elevation drops from 900m and 650 in Beit Sahour to 395m below sea level in the Dead Sea area. The short horizontal distance between highest and lowest elevation is only 25 km.

The atmosphere of Bethlehem is clear and its air is pure. Summer temperatures reach 35

Climate Chart

Average Maximun Temperatures (C°)

| | Bethlehem B | Hebron | | H |
| | Jericho | J | Nazareth | N |
	B	H	J	N
J	11	9	20	10
F	14	12	22	13
M	16	15	25	15
A	21	20	32	20
M	25	24	34	24
J	27	26	37	35
J	29	28	39	37
A	30	28	39	37
S	28	27	36	35
O	26	25	32	30
N	19	18	27	25
D	14	12	22	20

centigrade and in the winter temperature may drop to Zero. Bethlehem receives an average of 700 mm of rainfall annually. The inconsistency of rainfall across the months and years requires that most vegetable cultivation be supplemented with irrigation to ensure normal growth. The forested areas in the district comprise approximately 380 hectares. Most of these are located in the northwestern part of the district.

The rainy season starts in the second half of autumn (mid-October) and continues until the end of April. Heavy rain is, however, limited to fewer than 50 days, with around 70% of the rain falling during November to February. The town is influenced by the Mediterranean Sea breeze that comes around midday. However, the town is affected by annual waves of hot, dry, sandy and dust *Khamaseen* winds which originate from the Arabian desert during the months of April, May and mid-June.

Bethlehem receives an average of seven hours of sunshine a day during the Winter and thirteen hours during the Summer. As a consequence, Bethlehemites use roof-top solar collectors extensively, to capture the solar energy and to replace limited and expensive available energy resources.

The average annual relative humidity is 60% and reaches its highest rates during the months of January and February. In May, however, humidity levels are at their lowest. Night dew may occur in up to 180 days per year. Visitors are therefore advised to dress warmly in winter. While in summer, they are advised to bring light clothes and sweaters for the evening. In addition a head cover and sun block are essential for protection against sunstroke and sunburn.

Health:

It is advisable to bring your own medication including tablets and ointments that soothe stomach upsets, diarrhea, insect bites.

The medical services in Bethlehem are numerous and fairly well developed. Of the six hospitals in Bethlehem, three are maternity, one is psychiatric, one is pediatric and one is a general hospital. The total number of hospital beds is estimated at 506. There are 32 primary health care clinics in the Bethlehem district of which 16 are sponsored by NGO's (*non-governmental organizations*), 14 by private proprietary organizations, and two are associated with UNRWA. *(United Nations Relief Works Agency).* There are five ambulance vehicles and 133 physicians. In addition, there are 341 nurses and 27 dentists.

The district contains a large number of charitable societies and non-governmental organizations which offer health services unavailable in Palestine. A new wastewater collection network was recently constructed in the three towns of Bethlehem, Beit Jala and Beit Sahour. Approximately 99% of the population has access to drinkable piped water supply.

Hospital of the Holy Family

Caritas Baby Hospital

Other Hospitals:

1- **Al-Dibs Hospital**, Maternity
2- **Al-Hussein** Hospital, General
3- **Beit Sahour Cooperative Health Clinic**, Beit Sahour, Tel: 6475093 (24 hours).

Christian Benevolent Societies
Medical Institutions, clinics.

1. Women Child Care Society
P.O.B. 313, Beit Jala.
Near Orthodox Church
Tel: 742507, Fax: 742204

2. Holy Land Christian Mission
Mount David Orthopaedic Hospital.
Manger Street, P.O.B. 24
Tel: 742600, Fax: 741914

3. Knights of Malta
Hospital of the Holy Family Sisters of St. Vincent of Paul, P.O.B. 8. Tel: 741151, Fax: 741175

4. Beit Sahour Medical Center
P.O.B. 44, Beit Sahour, Tel: 6474443

5. Holy Family Care Center, Near Milk Grotto, P.O.B. 966, Tel: 6470002., Fax: 6470002

6. Caritas Baby Hospital, Pediatric, Tel: 741171

Public Transport System:

All special taxi fares are governed by a meter, which operates according to Tariff 1: 5:30 a.m. to 9 p.m.; tariff 2: 9:00 p.m. to 5.30 a.m. When starting a journey, the driver is obligated to activate the meter.

Shared taxis, *services*, run on particular routes between villages and towns. These are

Christian Institutions for Handicapped

1. Ephpheta Institute,
School for Audiophonetic rehabilitation of deaf children, Paul VI Street, P.O.B. 105.
Tel: 742568, Fax: 745576

2. House of Hope for the Blind and the Mentally Handicapped.
Hebron Road. P.O.B. 27 Across Ephpheta
Tel: 742325, Fax: 740928

3. Psychiatric Hospital of the Government
El-Jabal Street, Sisters of St. Dorothea, P.O.B. 60
Tel: 741155, Fax: 741657

4. Swedish International Relief Association (SIRA).
Special Education School, helps the slow learners. Beit Jala Road, P.O.B. 167. Tel: 742597, Fax: 741254

5. Siloah Mission
Rehabilitation Center for Physically Handicapped, P.O.B. 177, Beit Jala, Tel: 741373

6. Terre des Hommes
P.O.B. 20180, Tel: 742485, Fax: 747549

7. Bethlehem Arab Society for the Physically Handicapped
Cremisan Street, P.O.B. 100, Beit Jala, Tel: 744050, Fax: 744053

frequent and inexpensive. They set off from established spots around Bethlehem, one of which is the Manger Square. Another is al-Madbaseh Square. Negotiate with drivers for a trip off the established routes. A 7 seater stretch Mercedes can be hired with the driver for the day for U.S.$100. A good place to ask is the *As-Sha'b* Taxi office in the Manger Square, near the 'Umar Mosque.

Bethlehem has a limited bus service within the city and beyond. The bus lines are owned by private companies. A bus trip to Jerusalem costs approximately US$ 1.

Bus No. Dest. & Station

47	Beit Sahour, Manger Square
47	Jerusalem People's Market, Beit Sahour
22	Jerusalem Bus Station, Bethlehem
21	Jerusalem Beit Jala, Hebron Road
23	Hebron Hebron Road, Bab iz-qaq
39	Nahaline, Battir Cinema Sq. Bethlehem
B1	Solomon Pools Cinema Sq, Manger Sq.
B	Beit Jala Cinema Sq.
51	Beit Fajjar Cinema Sq.
60	St. Theodosios Bus Station, Bethlehem

Shared Taxi:

Destination	Station
Herodion	Peoples' Market, Beit Sahour.
Beit Sahour	Manger Square
Jerusalem	Manger Square
Beit Jala	Madbassah Sq.
Tequ'a	Qanah Str.

Car Rental

There are a number of car hire agencies in and around Bethlehem. You will need an international driving license and most agencies require you to be over 21 years old. Be cautious while driving for the streets are often narrow, permitting traffic in only one direction.

Murad Rent a Car	6470222
'Orabi Rent-a-Car	647 2004

Taxi

Manger Sq.	742647
As-Sha'b	742309
Hazboun	742647
Najmeh	742470
Beit Jala	742629
Shepherds Taxi	050 574292
Beit Sahour Taxi	050 586036
"	647 3363
"	050 352336
"	6472925

Airport Taxi Service:

In the mean time, International flights to the West Bank operate through Ben Gurion International Airport in Tel-Aviv, Israel, or through Queen Alia International Airport in Amman, Jordan.

Nesher: 24 hours service to and from Ben Gurion Airport. Tel: 6231231. It is advisable to make reservation 24 hours before flight. Egged Buses leave the airport for Jerusalem every twenty minutes.

Passport:

Visitors need a valid passport for entry into Bethlehem in the West Bank (under Israeli Administration), Israel or any other country, and a visa is stamped into it when entering the country. If you intend to use the same passport for visiting an Arab country (with the exception of Egypt and Jordan), ask the Israeli passport official to stamp your visa on the entry card rather than in you passport. Visitors are advised to contact the Embassy of the country they intend to visit before traveling.

The Working Week:

The working week is Saturday to Thursday. However, the mixed Muslim and Christian population means that Christian institutions and schools are closed on Sunday; Muslim institutions and schools are closed on Friday. However, you can find shops and restaurants open throughout the week. The general working hours are 8:00 a.m.- 4:00 p.m.; banks tend to close at around noon, and re-open in the afternoon from 3 pm. to 4.30 pm. Many shops stay open late into the night during the summer months and holiday seasons.

Muslim Holidays:

Muslim holidays are dated according to a lunar calendar, they fall on different days of the Gregorian calendar (Western one) in each year.

	1998	1999	2000
Ramadan	31/12	20/12	9/12
Eid al-Fitr	29/1	18/1	8/1
Eid al-Adha	7/4	27/3	16/3
Al-Hijra	27/4	17/4	5/4
Al-Mawlid	6/7	25/6	14/6
Hijra year	**1416/7**	**1417/8**	**1418/9**

Jewish holidays are dated also according to a lunar calendar, they fall on different days of the Gregorian calendar (Western one) in each year.

Palestinian Holidays:

International	
Women's Day	March 8
Land Day	March 30
Labor Day	May 1st
Independence Day:	Nov.15
Christmas	Dec. 25

Currency & Banks:

While the official currency is still the Israeli Shekel, the Jordanian Dinar is also widely used, though by no means accepted every where. It is also possible to use the U.S. Dollar in some shops and restaurants. Credit cards are accepted only in a limited number of shops and restaurants. Bethlehem has more than its fair share of legal Money Changers; walk down any street to find one. Following are the prevailing currency exchange rate against the New Israeli Shekel with little fluctuations:

	Buy	Sell
Jordanian Dinar	5.10	5.50
American Dollar	3.55	3.65
Deutsche Mark	2.08	2.10
French Franc	0.62	0.63
Sterling Pound	5.94	6.06

The exchange rate for hard currency in Money Changers offices is only marginally higher than the official bank rate.

Banks:

1. **Arab Bank**, Manger Street, Tel: 6470080
2. **Cairo-Amman Bank**, Manger Square, Tel: 744971,2,3
3. **The Land Bank**, Manger Square, Tel: 740860
4. **Jordan National Bank**, Manger Street, Tel: 6470951,2,3
5. **Palestine Investment Bank,** Nasser Street, Tel: 6470888.
6. **Bank of Jordan**. Will open soon.
7. **The Housing Bank**. Will open soon.

Banking Hours:
Saturday-Thursday: 8.30 a.m. to 12.30 p.m. 3 to 4 p.m.; except Thursday. Closed Fridays, religious and national holidays.

Media:

Bethlehem is home to three local television channels: *al-Mahd, ar-Ru'at, Bayt Lahm*, and a single radio station *Bethlehem 2000* which operates from Beit Sahour at 93.7 on the FM dial. Media infrastructure in Bethlehem is still in its early stages of development. The Palestinian Broadcasting Corporation operates small television station in Gaza and Ramallah which can be received in the Bethlehem area from a relay tower in Beit Jala. Private households in the area can also watch Israeli, Jordanian and Syrian TV and listen to Israeli, Jordanian, Syrian and Egyptian radios.

Two daily Arabic newspapers are sold in Bethlehem area, the largest is *al-Quds* with a circulation of 15,000 copies and *al-Hayat* newspaper. In addition, some six weekly and several monthly magazines are read by the inhabitants of Bethlehem. There is one weekly Palestinian newspaper in English, the *Jerusalem Times. The Jerusa-*

Local Codes:

02	Bethlehem, Hebron, Jerusalem, Jericho.
08	Lod, Ramleh, Ashdod.
09	Nablus, Qalqilya, Ramallah, Tulkarem, Natania.
07	Gaza, Khan Yunis, Rafah.
03	Ashqelon, Eilat, Jaffa, Tel Aviv.
04	Haifa, Akko, Naharia.
06	Nazareth, Tiberias, Safed, Afouleh.

lem Post is also available. Others are available upon request only.

Postal & Phone Services:

Christmas - Bethlehem 1996

The main post office in Bethlehem is in the Manger Square. It remains open continuously from 8:30 a.m. to 2:30 p.m. There is another branch on the Manger Street, near the Directorate of Education. It opens from 8:30 a.m. to 2:30 p.m.

Palestinian Stamps

Telephones:

The Bethlehem area has an extensive telephone network. There are several public card telephones. Phone cards can be bought at Post Offices and some shops. Several of the city's shops have coin phones which are fine for local calls, but expensive for long distance. Direct international calls can be placed at your hotel or the international telephone office in the Manger Square. The prefix for overseas calls to Bethlehem is: 972. The area code (02) is dialed without the zero. For example, (972 2 *the number*). The prefix for overseas calls from Bethlehem in 00, then you dial the international code of the country and your phone number.

Electric current:

The electric current used in Bethlehem is 220 volts AC, single phase, 50 Hertz. Three pin plugs are most commonly used, but some appliances utilize two-pin plugs. Electricity is supplied to the local power plant by the Jerusalem Electricity company.

Shopping Hours:

Souvenir shops are usually open all day from 9:00 a.m. to 7:00 p.m. without a break. The market place is open all day from 7:00 a.m. to 4:00 p.m. Other shops open all day from 9:00 a.m. to 5:00 p.m. with or without a short break at noon. At holiday seasons shops stay open for longer periods.

Souvenir Shops in Bethlehem

Manger Square

☞ Bamboo for Arts & Sculpture
Tel: 743937
☞ Bethlehem Oriental Store
Tel: 742812
☞ Holy Land Arts
Tel: 742835
☞ Jeries Freij & Sons Stores
Tel: 742888
☞ Issa Abu-Aita & Sons
Tel: 742911
☞ King David Store
Tel: 742474
☞ Lama Brothers
Tel: 743133, Fax: 742403
☞ Herodion Store
Tel: 742881, Fax: 741565
☞ Beit-Art Centre for Artisante
P.O:Box 1016
Telfax: 28 2323

Milk Grotto Street

☞ Bethlehem Star Store
Tel: 743297
☞ Lagrotto Souvenir Shop
Tel: 743461
☞ Milk Grotto Store
Tel: 745811
☞ Bethlehem Gift Store
Tel: 742736
☞ Do'q for Oriental Arts
Tel. 743663
☞ Holy Land Arts Museum
Tel: 744819
☞ The Nativity Store
Tel: 742678
☞ Treasure Store
Tel: 6470237
☞ Holy Land Souvenir
Tel: 743386
☞ Oriental Souvenir Store
Tel: 742328
☞ St. George Store
Tel: 742230

Manger Street

☞ Bethlehem Arts Gallery
Tel: 742368
☞ Halasa For Oriental Souvenirs, Tel: 743592
☞ Fatima Store
Tel: 742695, Fax: 743407
☞ Johnny's Souvenir
Tel: 744008

☞ Nisan Store
  Tel: 743589, Fax: 743985
☞ Saqa Brothers,
  Tel: 741313
☞ The Three Arches
  Tel: 742288, Fax: 742288
☞ The Good Shepherd Store
  Tel: 742249, Fax: 744544

Jerusalem -Hebron Road
☞ Canavati Store
  Tel: 741511, Fax: 741855
☞ Gallery Magus
  Tel & Fax: 6470417
☞ Hosh Olive Wood
  Tel: 743331, Fax: 741102

Beit Sahour
☞ Boaz's Field Souvenir Store,
  Tel: 6473605
☞ Holy Land Handicraft Coop.
  Beit Sahour, Tel: 744819,
  Fax: 6473088

Beit Jala
☞ Margo Zaidan
  (Hand-embroidered items)
  Tel: 741316

Dress:

When visiting Bethlehem, it is best to dress modestly. Basically this means no shorts, short skirts or sleeveless tops. While Bethlehem is one of the least conservative Palestinian towns, and you may see Palestinians showing more flesh than you, adherence to this simple rule is a good idea because it both respects local sensitivities and the same time staves off unwanted comments or harassment. This rule applies to visitors to the Nativity complex, and to other churches and mosques, not only in Bethlehem but elsewhere in Palestine.

Emergencies:

In case of emergency, contact any of these numbers for help or advice:

Police Station	748222
Emergency	741122
Fire Station	741123
Hussein Hospital	741161/2/3

Useful Telephone Numbers:

Overseas Operation	188
Time	155
Flight inquiries	9731111
Bethlehem Municipality	741323
Beit Sahour Municipality	6473666
Beit Jala Municipality	742601
Chamber of Commerce	742742,
Fax	741327
Allenby Bridge	9943358,
	9922500
Skeikh Hussein Bridge	
Israeli Border	03-966885
Jordanian Border	962637524

Palestinian National Authority
(Tel & Fax)

President Office
7-824670, Fax 07-822366
International Cooperation
2-5747045, 02-5744044
Internal Affairs
7-864174, 07-862500
Health
7-829179, 07-869809
Public Works
7-865900, 07-829272
Housing
7-822233, 07-822318
Economy
2-5747040, 02-5747041
Labor
2-9922616, 02-9921270
Information
2-9954041, 02-9954043
Finance
07-829243, 07-820696
Education
02-9985555, 02-9985559
Justice
07-823460, 07-867109
Religious Affairs

02-284886, 02-282085
Youth Affairs
02-9985982, 02-9985991
Tourism
02-741581, 02-741327
Telecommunication
02-9923211, 02-9922233
Agriculture
07-829124, 02-9921280
Local Government
02-9922619, 02-9921240
Culture
02-9986205, 02-9986204
Jerusalem Affairs
02-273573, 02-274020
Civil Affairs
02-9985901, 02-9956047

Diplomatic Missions at the PNA (Palestinian National Authority)

Danish	9923193
Dutch	611560
Egyptian	07-824290
German	9921044
Jordanian	07-829476
Moroccan	07-822583
Norwegian	07-821902

Consulates in Jerusalem

Belgium	828263
Denmark	258083
France	259481
Greece	619583
Spain	828006
Sweden	828117
Turkey	321087
UK	828281
USA	253288

Other Charitable Institutions, Unions and Clubs in the Area: BL Bethlehem, BJ Beit Jala, BS Beit Sahour

Al-Aman Counselling Center, BL Tel: 741190
Al-Alaa'eya School for the Blind BL, Tel:744211
Al-Ihsan Society
Al-Wafa Society

Applied Research Institute, BL
Caritas Street. P.O.B. 860,
Tel & Fax: 741889.
Internet: envir@arij.pl.org.
Arab Women' Union
BL, Tel: 742559, BJ, BS
Al-Thakafi Club, Beit Sahour
Al-Muntada al-Thaqafi, BL
Tel: 742826
Alternative Information Center
Tel: 747854
Assyrian Orthdox Club BL Tel: 742805
Arab Benevolent Society, BJ Tel: 742268
Artas Folklore Center, P.O.B. 746
Beit Jala Nusing Home 741664
Battir Charitable Society
Catholic Action Club, BL
Tel: 743277
Communal Society for Mental Health, BL Tel: 744848
Carpet of Mercy Society
Defense of the Children Int'l
Tel: 050305711
DATA, Manger St.
Tel: 743343, Fax: 743369
Family Development Society
Friend of the Patients 742415
Handicrafts Training Workshop
Society for Girls
Holy Land Handicraft
Cooperation Souvenir Shop
Ibrahimieh Society
Infant Welfare Society
Islamic Charitable Society
Islamic *Zakat* Committee
Islamic Club, Bethlehem
Jemima-Home for Handicapped Children, BJ Tel: 741214
Life Gate (Rehab Center) 741373
Ladies Annoint Society, BL
National Orthodox Society
Orthodox Charitable Society,
Beit Jala Tel: 742398
Orthodox Club, Bethlehem,
Beit Jala,   Tel: 745097
Beit Sahour,   Tel: 6472247
Saint-Afram Assyrian Orth. Soc.
BL, Tel: 742767
St. Yves Society (legal aid) Tel: 747603

Red Cross Int'l Committee
Tel: 743225
Wifaq' Center for Conflict Resolution.
Women's Vocational Training Society
YMCA
Young Ladies' Rehab Workshop, BL Tel: 742696
Za'tara Charitable Society

**Christian Homes
for the Elderly**

1. Antonian Society, Sister of Hortus Conclusus

The Antonian Society

Caritas Street, P.O.B. 35
Tel: 742573, Fax: 742573

2. Charitable Society for the Aged
P.O.B. 38, Beit Jala
Tel: 740893, Fax: 742772

Christian Homes for Children:

1. Crêche-Children Home
Sisters of Charity,
Tel: 744142, Fax: 744142

2. Holy Family Hospital
Sisters of Charity, P.O.B. 8,
Tel: 741151, Fax: 741154

3. Sisters of Hortus Conclusus
P.O.B. 6, Tel: 742427

4. S.O.S. Children Village
El Karkafa Street, P.O.B. 137
Tel: 742267, Fax: 745179

5. Talitha Kumi College
(Boarding Section), Talitha Kumi Street, P.O.B. 7, Biet Jala, Tel: 741247, Fax: 741847

Hotels:

There are several hotels and guest houses in the Bethlehem Area. The majority are a few minutes walk from the Manger Square. Rooms with single, double, or three beds are available for US$30, 50, 70 per night. Breakfast is included. The ratings as expressed by the number of stars represent both the atmosphere of the hotel and the general treatment. Accommodation in Bethlehem is under-priced in comparison to Jerusalem. Bethlehem is booked out at Christmas and Easter. At these times it's advisable to book well in advance, although you can usually find a bed somewhere less popular.

Manger Square:

Orient Palace Hotel
Tel: 742728, Fax: 741562
Eastern & Western food.

Palace Hotel

Guest House Hotel ☆☆
Tel: (9720 2 741348
Fax: (972) 2 742280
Eastern & Western food

Manger Street:

Alexander Hotel ☆☆☆
Tel: (972) 2 6470780/1
Fax: (972) 2 6470048
Eastern food

Paradise Hotel

Paradise Hotel ☆☆☆☆
Tel: (972) 2 744542/3
Fax: (972) 2 744544
Eastern & Western food

Bethlehem Hotel

Bethlehem Hotel ☆☆☆
Tel: (972) 2 6470702
Fax: (972) 2 6470706
Eastern & Western food

Paul VI Street:

Grand Hotel ☆☆☆
Tel: (972) 2 741440
Fax: (972) 2 741604
Eastern & Western food

Bethlehem Inn ☆☆
Caritas Str., Tel: (972) 2 742423,
Fax: 742424
Eastern & Western food

Bethlehem Star Hotel ☆☆☆
Frères Street
Tel: (972) 2 6470285

Grand Hotel

Fax: (972) 2 741494
Eastern food

Shepherd Hotel ☆☆
Naser Street
Tel: (972) 2 740656
Fax: (972) 2 744888
Eastern & Western food

St. Antonio Hotel ☆☆
Saqa Quarter
Tel and Fax: (972) 2 6470524
Eastern & Western food

Beit Jala

Al-Mahd Hotel ☆☆☆
(Nativity Hotel)

Nativity Hotel

As-Sahl Street
Tel: (972) 2-6470650
Fax: (972) 2 744083
Eastern & Western food

Star Hotel

Christian Guest Houses in Bethlehem Area

Christian hospices generally offer facilities much like those of the better hostels for similar prices, but they're geared primarily to Christian pilgrims and usually located in convents.

1. Abu Gubran,
Lutheran Guest House,
Paul VI Street, P.O.B. 162
Tel: 6472312, Fax: 6470048
Eastern food

2. Beit El-Baraka
Hebron Road, P.O.B. 1
Tel: 9929299, Fax: 9929288

3. Casa Nova
Manger Square, P.O.B. 996
Tel: 743981, Fax: 743540
Italian & Western food

4. Franciscans of Mary, White Sisters
Milk Grotto Street P.O.B. 11

St. Joseph's Home

Tel: 742441, French food.

5. Foyer Mar Charbel
Wadi Ma'ali Road, P.O.B. 665
Tel: 742155, Fax: 6472821
Lebanese food.

6. Saint Joseph's Home
Manger Street, P.O.B. 199
Tel: 6470155, Fax: 6470334

7. Talitha Kumi Hostel
P.O.B. 7, Beit Jala
Tel: 741247, Fax: 741847
Eastern food.

8. Betharam Pilgrims Center
Maison de Betharam
P.O.Box 170,
Western food.

BASIC TEERMS IN ARABIC

Days of the Week

Sunday	youm el-had
Monday	youm el-itneen
Tuesday	youm el-talaata
Wednesday	youm el-arba'a
Thursday	youm el-khamees
Friday	youm el-Jum'a
Saturday	youm es-sabt

Numbers:

1	Wahed
2	itneen
3	thalata
4	arab'a
5	khamsah
6	sitta
7	sab'a
8	thamanya
9	tis'a
10	'ashara
100	miya
1000	alef
First	awal
Last	akhir
Next	ittani

Food:

Water	maya
Milk	haleeb
Bread	khubez
Cheese	jibneh
Salt	meleh

Sugar	sukar
Tea	shai
Coffee	qahwa
Meat	lahmah
Fish	samak
Fruit	fawakeh
Glass	kas
Fork	shokeh
Knife	sikineh
Spoon	mal'aqa
Plate	sahin
Kilo	kilo
Half	nus
Quarter	rub'
Table	tawleh
Chair	kursi
Hungry	jaw'aan
Thirsty	'atshaan
The bill	al-Hissab

Other terms:

Yes	na'am
No	laa
Hello	marhaba
Sorry	asif
Never mind	ma'alesh
Where is	wain fi
Hotel	otel
Restaurant	mat'aam
Post office	al-bareed
Toilet	el-hamam
Shop	dukan
Left	shimal
Right	yameen
Straight	dughri
Near	qareeb
Far	ba'id
Up	fouk
Down	tahat
Here	hoon
There	honak
When	mata
Today	el-yom
Tomorrow	bukra
God willing	insha' allah
Thank God	al hamdou lilah
How much	qadeesh
It's too much	hada ktir
Expensive	ghali
Do you have?	fi 'andak
There is	fi
There isn't	ma feesh

l don't want	bideesh
I'm tired	ana ta'ban
Please	min fadlak
Thank you	shukran

Expressions:

How are your?	keef halak
Fine	mabsut
You're welcome	ahlan wa sahlan
Goodbye	bi-khatrak
Goodbye (response)	ma' salameh
Good morning	sabah el-kheer
Good evening	masa el-kheer
Good night	leleh sa'ydah
What is your name?	shu ismak
My name	ismi
Do you speak English?	bitehki inglizi
A little	shwaiyeh
How do you say	keef bitqul
Where is the bus?	wain el bus
Everything's OK	kulshay tamaam
I don't understand	mush fahim

BOOKS

There are possibly more books written about Bethlehem than about any other city in the Holy Land. They range from early travel writings to ancient and modern histories, religion and archaeology. The following is a list of the most important books:

Dalman, Gustaf. **Sacred Sites and Ways.** London, Society for Promoting Christian Knowledge, 1935

Dory, Vincent. **Bethléem**. Imprimerie Edouard Dory. Bruxelles, 1901.

El-Ali, **Geries. Bethlehem the Immortal Town**. Jerusalem, 1991.

Faber, Fredrick. **Bethlehem**. The Peter Reilly Co. Philadephia, 1955.

Franciscan in Bethlehem, 1347-1947. Franciscan Printing Press, Jerusalem, 1947.

Hamilton, R.W. **The Church of the Nativity, Bethlehem,** Jerusalem, 1947

Hamilton, R.W. **A Guide to Bethlehem,** Jerusalem, Azriel Press,1939

Harvey, William. **Structural Survey of the Church of the Nativity, Bethlehem.** Oxford University Press, London 1935

Harvey, W. & Others. **The Church of Nativity at Bethlehem**. London, 1910.

Hintlian, George, Bargil Pixner, A. Van der Heyden. **The Glory of Bethlehem.** Jerusalem, Jerusalem Publishing House, 1981

Hoade, Eugene. O.F.M. **Guide to the Holy Land.** Jerusalem, Franciscan Printing Press, 1996.

Isaac, Jad. **Environmental Profile for Bethlehem.** Applied Research Institute, Bethlehem, 1995.

Luke, Harry Charles. **A Guide to Jerusalem and Judea.** The Traveler's Handbook for Palestine and Syria. London, Simpkin,1924

Nazzal, Jamil & Afif Boulos. **Path-Finder Guide to Palestine, Transjordan & Syria.** Jerusalem: The Palestine Educational Co. 1934

Perowne, Stewart. **The Pilgrim's Companion in Jerusalem and Bethlehem**. Hodder and Staughton.

Pictorial Guide to Bethlehem. Franciscan Printing Press, Jerusalem, 1988.

Petrozzi, Maria Teresa. **Bethlehem**. Translated by Godfrey Kloetzly O.F.M. Franciscan Printing Press, Jerusalem

Porter, J.L. **Jerusalem, Bethany and Bethlehem.** Ariel Publishing Co. Jerusalem, 1886.

L"Archiconfrerie du Très Saint Enfant Jesus de Bethléem, Essai Historique, Rome, 1958

Lemaire, R.P. Paulin, O.F.M. **Petit Guide de Terre Sainte.** Jerusalem, Imprimerie des PP. Franciscains, 1956

Zev Vilany. **Steimatzky's Palestine Guide.** General Survey by Dr. A Bonne. Jerusalem, 1941

Rene Burri. **In search of the Holy Land.** Eyre Methuen, London 1979

Vionnet, M. **Les Eglises de la Nativite à Bethléem**. Byzantion, Tom XIII, 1938.

Books on Food:

Roden, Claudia. **A Book of Middle Eastern Food**. Penguin Books. 1984.

Nickles, Harry. **Middle Eastern Cooking**. Time-Life Books. New York, 1969.

List of Main Churches

Greek-Orthodox

Nativity Church
  Tel: 742440
St. Nicolas' Church
  Tel:741020,
St. George's Church
  Tel: 74102
Mar Elias' Church,
  Tel:6760966
St. George's Church,
  al-Khadr, Tel:743233
Church of St. Sabas, Mar Sabas
Church of St.Theodosios
  Ibn 'Ubaid Tel: 050282447
Shepherds' Field Church
  Beit-Sahour, Tel:6473135
Greek Orthodox Church
  Beit-Sahour, Tel: 6471483
Church of the Virgin
  Beit-Jala, Tel: 050445255
Church of St. Nicola
  Beit-Jala, Tel: 050445255
Syriac Orthodox church
  Paul VI Street.Tel:744757

Armenian - Orthodox

St. Jacob's Church
  Manger Square, Tel: 742410
Northern Transept Church
  Basilica, Tel 742410

The Catholic Churches

St. Catherine Parish Church
  Manger Sq. Tel: 742425
Holy Manger, Nativity Church,
  Tel:742425
Caritas Baby Hospital
  Caritas Street, Tel 741171
Salesian Fathers-Sacred Heart.
  Tel: 742421
Maronite Church
  Qanat Street, Tel:742155
Milk Grotto Chapel
  Milk Grotto Str. Tel:743867
St. Joseph's Chapel,
  al-Atan, Tel:742425
St. Luios Chapel - Salesian
  Madbasah Square, Tel:742421

Carmelite Church
  Nasir's Street, Tel:742486
Bethlehem University Chapel
  Freres Street, Tel:743151
Emmanuel Nuns' Chapel
  Caritas Street.Tel:742800
The White Nuns' Chapel
  Milk Grotto St. Tel:743876
Shepherds' Field Church
  Beit-Sahour, Tel: 6472413
Latin Church,
  Beit-Sahour, Tel:6472733
Franciscan Nuns' Chapel
  Aida - Beit-Jala, Tel:742792
Gremesan Convent Chapel
  Beit-Jala, Tel:742605
Syrian Catholic Church
  Manger Street, Tel: 742497
Creek Catholic Church
  Star Street, Tel:742493
Greek Catholic Church
  Beit-Sahour, Tel: 6472424
Greek Catholic Seminary
  Beit-Sahour, Tel:6472424

Lutheran Church

Lutheran Nativity Church
  Bethlehem, Tel:6470047
Lutheran Evangelical Church
  Beit Sahour,Tel: 6472720,
Lutheran Evangelical Church
  Beit Jala, Tel : 742613
First Baptist Church
  Caritas Street, Tel:741930
Local Baptist Church
  Bab-iz-qaq, Tel: 741820
Baraka Bible Presbyt. Church
  Tel: 742480
Church of God
  Beit Jala Tel: 050 311100

The Ethiopian

Ethiopian Church
  Milk Grotto Str. Tel:744204

The Copts:

Church of the Virgin
  Milk Grotto Street